BEYOND NEGATIVE THINKING

BREAKING THE CYCLE OF DEPRESSING AND ANXIOUS THOUGHTS

BEYOND NEGATIVE THINKING

BREAKING THE CYCLE OF DEPRESSING AND ANXIOUS THOUGHTS

JOSEPH T. MARTORANO, M.D.
AND
JOHN P. KILDAHL, PH.D.

PERSEUS PUBLISHING
Cambridge, Massachusetts

Library of Congress Cataloging in Publication Data

Martorano, Joseph T.
  Beyond negative thinking: breaking the cycle of depressing and anxious
thoughts / Joseph T. Martorano and John P. Kildahl.
      p.   cm.
  Includes bibliographical references and index.
  ISBN 0-306-43196-3
  1. Negativism. 2. Self-talk. 3. Cognitive therapy. I. Kildahl, John P. II. Title.
BF698.35.N44M37   1989   89-7583
153.4′2—dc20   CIP

ISBN   0738206172

10   9   8   7   6   5   4   3   2

Names, places, and other identifying facts contained
herein have been fictionalized, and no similarity to
any persons, living or dead, is intended.

Published by Perseus Publishing
A Member of the Perseus Books Group

An Insight Book

Printed in the United States of America

PREFACE

Why does traditional psychotherapy take so long?

In a world where everything is moving faster, can't we find a way to effect psychological change that doesn't run into years and cost a fortune?

This was the prime question we asked ourselves during our combined half-century of clinical experience in psychiatry and clinical psychology.

First of all, we began to synthesize our knowledge about various schools of psychotherapy with the emerging data from the new science of thinking, or cognition. We devoted particularly close study to the process by which individuals achieve personal change. The bottom line seemed to be this:

Ask someone how his life has changed for the better and one thing you will be sure to hear is *"my thinking has changed."*

This synopsis led us to experiment with a therapeutic design that would help people *change their thinking* from the very outset of their psychotherapy. Research on thinking was discovering that *thoughts pre-*

ceded feelings. Many traditional therapies had focused on the *by-products* of thinking—that is, the feelings and behavior of the patient. What seemed a direct approach—after all, what is more immediate than what we feel or how we act?—turns out to be an oblique one. Probably nobody ever claimed that feelings and behavior are the royal road to insight—but, in fact, traditional psychotherapy was going by way of Troy!

Naturally, then, meaningful change took long to accomplish. Habitual, but often unnoticed thought patterns were given too little weight. People forty years old were making the same mistakes they made at fourteen. Their lives may have seen a dramatic run of events—career successes and setbacks, marriage, family, divorce; but the basic pattern of their lives—withdrawal, negativism, depression—persisted due to the same thought patterns that produced their feelings.

The key to changing feelings and behavior is to change how and what one thinks. Nearly all our patients asserted that they could think anything they wanted to think. After all, we're all capable of thinking for ourselves, aren't we? Nobody's brainwashing us, nobody's playing with our minds. Theoretically, at least, then, our patients should be able to feel however they chose to feel—since their feelings were the end product of the very thoughts they chose to think, and over which they took mastery for granted.

In this logical sequence, obviously, there seemed to be many a slip. But further research and psychotherapy experience showed us that thought processes could be accessed directly: for thinking is made up of words, *is* "inner speech." We were able to demonstrate that people *could* control their inner speech, their word-thoughts. Their problem was that they generally pushed all the wrong buttons. And the choice of thoughts — often a wrong choice — determined what feelings would follow. People needed help in choosing the thoughts that were in their own best interests. At this they balked. Thoughts must be *"true."* And the truth must be against them. Truth is negative. How else can you tell it's true? Thus ran the consensus of "thinking on thinking."

We had our work cut out for us. Early results with patients led to some successes. We formed the basis for a system that people could understand, take home with them, and practice by themselves to produce clear-cut results. This was only the beginning. We kept fine-tuning the system until we had structured five distinct progressive steps in individual thinking that in turn produced sustained transformation in feeling. We related these thinking changes to more effective behavior and, in time, to an overall happier life for the individual.

Joseph T. Martorano
John P. Kildahl

INTRODUCTION

HOW YOU CAN BENEFIT FROM INNER SPEECH TRAINING

The growth of the human mind is still
high adventure, in many ways, the high-
est adventure on earth.
                                        Norman Cousins

Everyone knows a story of someone's therapy that
didn't quite work. Maybe it wasn't totally ineffective
but it cost too much for what the person got out of it.
Perhaps the patient found it comforting to have someone to talk to week after week, but nothing much
changed. Or, it could have been the type of treatment
where the patient lay on the couch and free-associated
for five 50-minute sessions per week, and heard hardly
anything from the analyst at all.

What went wrong? The old therapies were seduc-
tive, but just telling someone how you feel is not
enough. Psychoanalytic theories are fascinating. Free
association is intriguing. But as treatments for helping
people in need, many of the old therapies are inefficient, not cost-effective.

3

Dramatic advances in research have led to new therapies which much more rapidly get at the underlying causes of emotional problems, and then offer direct solutions. These new studies have led to a new understanding of thinking, feelings, and behavior, and how to change and improve them. In every science, each decade brings breakthroughs that build on past advances. That has happened in the field of psychotherapy.

Cognitive therapy (literally, "thinking therapy") is a result of this research.

This new cognitive therapy is accessible to everyone. You do not need to be a student of psychology to understand how to change your life. You can use the five specific, practical, and jargon-free techniques described in this book to make significant changes in your thinking, and therefore, in your life.

How can this be?

First, thinking is now *a measurable process*. The brain is more active than formerly believed and new computerized instruments can review and record precise information about what happens in the brain when someone is thinking.

Second, *thinking precedes feeling*. This is a fundamental finding from brain research. What does it mean for you? It means that if you want to feel better, and have a better life, the crucial question is not "How are you feeling?" but "What are you thinking? What were you thinking that *caused* your feeling?" For your thoughts precede and therefore produce your feelings.

If you are in psychotherapy treatment, or have ever been in therapy, review in your mind a session you remember. How much time did you spend talking about your feelings? Then ask yourself how much time you spent talking about your thoughts behind your feelings.

You need to identify the thought behind the feeling if you want to stop repeating the same old errors over and over again. You do not have to be passive about your therapy or your life. *You* have the best access to your own thoughts, and you can actively study your thoughts and thereby improve your feelings and your life. The Inner Speech System gives you the guidelines to do this.

Third, your thinking is not automatic. You can change your thoughts. You can improve your thoughts on a permanent basis. Someone once said, "The brain is only as strong as its weakest think."

It will be helpful for you to follow a system to help you step outside your mind, and see exactly how to change your thinking. This is the system the authors have designed as a result of their combined half-century of practical, clinical experience with people.

This system starts with the cause of people's problems—their thinking. When your thinking is changed to become more effective, the symptom of weak thinking, namely your feelings, will change. As you probably already know, it is virtually impossible to correct the feeling through just working on the feelings. But when you reconstruct the underlying *thought,* change takes place.

Power Thinking has the advantage of standing on the shoulders of many scholars, researchers, practitioners, and authors. We have studied the best of them, and have tried to fine-tune the factors that make all therapies effective. Contributions from psychoanalysis, neo-Freudianism, existential and humanistic psychologies, behavior therapy, ego psychology, object relations, and others can be seen as forming the foundations of our theories in this volume. Of special relevance to us is the "Voice Therapy" developed by Robert W. Firestone.

In the field of cognitive psychotherapy, Donald Meichenbaum, Albert Ellis, Aaron Beck, Wayne Dyer, and David Burns are among the many psychologists and psychiatrists who have led the way with their research and writing. Their work is now the foundation of many projects, ranging from brief magazine articles to major governmental studies. Cognitive therapy has entered the mainstream of American culture.

Yet cognitive therapy is by no means the only effective therapy. Tastes in therapy, as in everything, vary, and satisfaction comes in different forms for differing people. We do not exclude other theories and therapies in our own approach. But we do know from decades of practice that cognitive therapy provides powerful forces for change and growth in every branch of the therapeutic spectrum.

If you listen to the description of any successful therapeutic experience, of whatever form of therapy, you can be sure that the patient has somehow learned to think differently. When patients *think* differently, they *feel* differently—and they *act* differently.

You can control what you think about, once you learn how to do it.

John Milton wrote, "The mind is its own place, and in itself can make a heaven of hell, a hell of heaven."

The choice is yours.

CHAPTER 1

INNER SPEECH TRAINING
FIVE TECHNIQUES THAT CAN
CHANGE YOUR THINKING

How often have you had a thought like —

"With *my* kind of *luck* —"
"*All my life, nothing's* panned out."
"Nothing *ever* goes like I planned."
"Where does it leave me *if* — ?"
"I'll *never* meet the right person."
"I *always* screw up."

How do such *thoughts* make you *feel*?

Do they contribute to your fulfillment, your happiness, satisfaction, health, success, or to helping people around you feel hopeful?

After all, if your own mind isn't on your side, who's going to come out *for* you?

Can you learn to make your thoughts work *for*, rather than against you? If thoughts can make you feel defeated and bitter, can you alter your thoughts so that you feel confident, pleased at things you've accomplished, and at new possibilities ahead? Certainly, if your thoughts can turn your feelings one way, they can lead them in a different direction. To *feel* better, you should *think* better.

By applying five simple, practical thinking techniques, you can learn to become the master instead of the victim of your thoughts and feelings. These techniques are:

1. *Listening In.* Training to hear yourself thinking.
2. *Underlining.* Selecting the specific words in your internal dialogue that are detrimental to you and your own best interests.
3. *Stopping.* Shutting off the negative words in your internal thought speech.
4. *Switching.* Interrupting harmful inner speech and substituting positive internal voices.
5. *Reorienting.* Changing the thrust of your thinking to an active, problem-solving mode.

WHAT IS THINKING?

Your thinking, your feelings—in fact, your entire consciousness—is based upon the words and the combinations of words you have learned to use. You form your thoughts by choosing words. That is Inner Speech.

A word is the *smallest* possible unit of *communication.* Try to achieve anything beyond the simplest communication without words. It is very difficult. We may be able to experience non-word, complex visual or abstract thoughts, but in order to *communicate* our thoughts—even to *ourselves*—words are all we've got.

Indeed, even when we are just communicating to ourselves, our words form a *dialogue*, as if *we are talking to ourselves.*

Thinking is inner speech. To think is to speak silently, *internally*—an inner voice is repeating the words on this page as you read them.

As you read, you have the opportunity to analyze your thinking. Listen In to your inner speech as you make your way across a page. The words in print are transcribed into inner speech. The sentences are repeated in your mind. Inner speech is the experience of thinking. Your brain also develops its own thoughts as you read. You hear an internalization of your own voice talking to yourself as you produce your inner response to the page before your eyes. ("Right, right—I've done that."—"Maybe not *that*, but what *I* do is worse.")

A revealing experiment is to take a quiet few minutes alone, sit down comfortably, and tune in to your mind. Do you hear a stream of words, phrases, whole sentences, jangling, jibing, warning, rehashing, nagging, often beleaguering you? With thoughts like these, who needs enemies? Like all Inner Voices, yours has been piling up negative messages for years. "You know you're absentminded."—that's your mother. "The trouble with you is you think there are forty-eight hours in every day, fourteen days..."—your father. "It's funny that all the rest of the class heard me!"—Ms. Gaffney, your fifth-grade teacher. Your Inner Voice absorbed them all, and now it plays them back to you like a nonstop tape. The theme is that *only you* forget, fudge, fail, and that is all you can be counted on for. Your Inner Voice harps on regrets and recriminations, worries, and fears. And it transfers them all to you, speaking to you and for you. "I should have spoken up, but I'm so chicken." "It was crazy of me to get enraged at Alison." "I know I"ll blow that test." "Ron's been so *considerate* lately. Has he got something going with that new lady in Material Control?"

Do these sound anything like some thoughts you think? If they do, this is not some aberration on your part; it's a quite standard state of affairs. Our minds are at work 24 hours a day, asleep or awake, and like it or not, we're profoundly affected by whatever thoughts fill our minds. If those messages spell gloom and doom, that's where we're headed. More literally than we have ever imagined, we travel through life with our thoughts as navigator, and we veer in whichever direction they guide us.

WHAT IS HEALTHY THINKING?

All of this obtaining and processing of information by your brain into thoughts and feelings seem to go on quite automatically or unconsciously. Unfortunately, sometimes your mind is programmed like the voice of an antagonistic commentator or parents. The kind of parents who believed it was their job to create a perfect specimen—morally, mentally, and physically—and not of the person we are, but of one *they* may have wished to be—perhaps one who never was. Then the language of your inner speech, instead of coming out for you, as it always should, may undermine or actually sabotage your desire to be confident, secure, and happy. Insidious inner speech damages everything you do.

Inner Speech Training is the method by which you control the words in your head that are used in the formation of your thoughts, and direct these words, and therefore your thoughts, in a positive and profitable direction.

HOW DO YOU BECOME A WELL-TRAINED THINKER?

The five techniques that have been set forth—*Listening In, Underlining, Stopping, Switching,* and *Reorienting*—can be mastered one by one. This system of Inner Speech Training can help you to become a thinker who finds his thoughts his best resource, not one who wants to run from them.

This method is an alternative to feeling as though your inner speech is beyond your control. Through Inner Speech Training you can identify particular problem areas in your thinking. Once you've learned where the problem areas are, you'll learn specific techniques to stop these unwanted voices. When you've mastered stopping your unwanted thought patterns, you can learn to tune the voices inside your head until you control them so that they speak only at your command. And when they do speak, they will be *yours*, not the voices of your detractors, or the voices of the past.

As you become aware of your internal voice or voices, you will realize that Internal Speech shapes your life more than any other single force. This may well sound familiar; the Book of Proverbs says: "As a man thinketh in his heart, so is he."

Inner Speech Training is a new technique similar to what therapists call "cognitive restructuring." These therapies, including I.S.T., work by changing the basic way your mind perceives and shapes events. They are user-friendly, and can supplement whatever form of therapy and self-help that works well for you.

LISTENING IN TO YOUR INTERNAL VOICES

Is your thinking a meeting of committees? Are your thoughts dominated by dissenting factions that all have to have their say and keep you from getting on to more pleasurable living and productive activities? The *Grievance Committee* is one that tends to convene often and run late; just to remind you how you're pushed around:

"I don't have to take
this garbage."

"It would be one thing
if I was getting paid
what I'm worth."

"I'm through covering
for her after the way
she bad-mouthed me."

Then there's the *Committee for Self-Criticism*, that aims to keep you on your toes:

"If I could just keep
my big mouth shut."

"I get too upset."

"I'm not into other
people enough."

"I get on people's
nerves. I rub them the
wrong way."

Or the *Committee of Regrets*:

"If I could just go back
and do it over."

"I wish I hadn't said anything."

"I didn't know when I was well off."

"I could have handled it differently."

Is your mind filled with unending dialogues?

Are there voices in your head right now anxiously preparing future discussions with your friends, your spouse, your boss, a parent, or teacher?

Are you forever listening in to these discussions so that you can't concentrate on the real things going on around you?

Is your mind overpreparing each coming event by endlessly mulling over all the possibilities for what might occur?

"What will I do if he says he wants to cool it?"

"What will I do if she says it isn't working out?"

"What if Davis quits? He's my real backer in the office."

Or is your mind a battlefield, constantly filled with explosions?

"I should have punched him out."

"Why didn't I tell him
to shove it?"

Some inner voices tear us down, other voices keep
saying, in various ways, "What's the use?" And we consider that this is dealing with "reality," "*facing* it." Some
inner voices are not even our own, but are other people's thoughts and feelings taking over our thoughts.

Learning *how you think* could be the most important thing you can do to prepare yourself for the rest of
your life.

HOW DOES YOUR THINKING WORK?

All productive thinking is done in the form of Internal Speech—either monologues or dialogues that
you experience as *voices* in the middle of your head
(your Internal Speech Center). Most of your thinking
takes the form of a dialogue. Word-thoughts make up
most of your thinking.

Example:

Do you ever think...?

What will I do
if...   ...when I get there
                                 Mrs. Howard says,
                                 "Oh, we meant *next*
                                 Thursday!"?

                                 ...the elevator gets
                                 stuck?

These word-thoughts are linked together to form dialogues.
The dialogue is experienced as *Inner Speech* to yourself
or a dialogue between yourself and someone else.

"Should I keep going out with him? He's *nice*,...but he doesn't turn me on." (your voice)

"Yes, you go into the woods looking for a straight stick and you come out with a crooked one!" (Mother's voice)

INNER SPEECH TRAINING

Inner Speech Training—I.S.T.—is a system to help you learn to improve how you think. I.S.T.

Enables you to repattern the entire set of your mind;

Identifies the *cause*, not the symptom (feelings and behavior are resulting symptoms);

Provides a guide to *permanent change* by attacking the problems *at their point of origin* in your mind;

Unlocks the *secrets* of *how* you think and gives you effective techniques to deal with problem areas;

Allows you to achieve mastery over your feelings and your behavior by attacking the source of the difficulties in your mind;

Gives you control over the *tyrannical voices* you may hear in your head, voices that have prevented your becoming an independent person.

The Inner Speech Training system builds on the facts that

you think in words;

your thinking produces
   your feelings
   and
   your actions; and
the words and phrases of your mind select the building blocks of
   your thinking,
   your feeling,
   and
   your actions.

If you tend to use the same words in your thoughts, you will tend to feel always the same way, and act the same way.

If you think in clichés, your actions will also be stereotypic.

If you think in tired old words, you will feel and act in tired old ways.

If you select different, unusual words, you create the possibility that you will feel and act in a new way. If you use upbeat words, you increase your chances of feeling and acting optimistically. If you choose power words with vitality in them, you will be more apt to feel and act enthusiastically and purposefully.

Here is how to feel *worse*:

A patient called. She said,
   "I got some bad news."
   "What happened?"
   "The doctor said the x-rays didn't look good."

"What exactly did your doctor say?"

"He said, 'The x-rays don't look too bad.' See? Something's wrong."

Or visualize two people in their fifties:

A. "I really feel old."

B. "I feel like I finally grew up. I really feel mature."

Try repeating each of the last two comments. Both of them acknowledge the passage of time. Neither one "quarrels with the rules of the game." B doesn't say, "Life begins at fifty-seven." But the statements feel different by the shading of the words. "Old" means "I've had it." "Mature" means "I can cope."

That's how much difference your choice of words in your internal speech can make to you.

The following chapters describe the five steps by which you can train yourself to think more powerfully.

CHAPTER 2

THE CASE OF AMY
HER FIRST EXPERIENCE WITH INNER SPEECH TRAINING

The first thing Amy said when she came in the office and sat down was, "I know you can't do anything for me, Doctor. I don't want you to feel bad about it." Amy's second remark was, "I'm a total mess. I've screwed up everything in my life. I've tried everything. Nothing helped."

Her new therapist asked her to tell more about herself.

"Things are going down the tubes at work. I keep lousing up, and I'm sure I'm going to be canned. My personal life is more of the same. Don—the guy I've been seeing—hasn't called for three days. He must be seeing someone else."

Amy put herself down ten consecutive times in the first ten sentences she spoke. Gradually, her story moved past the putdowns. Amy was twenty-eight. She had received her MBA two years ago, and was already making $40,000 a year. That didn't seem like a total screw-up. What had gone wrong with Don?

She really didn't know, she said. They had been seeing each other with increasing frequency for the better part of a year. They hadn't had a fight or any kind of "discussion." In fact, everything had seemed great. He kissed her good night like always. And yet, it hadn't occurred to Amy to call Don to check if he was okay. Instead, she jumped to the conclusion that in three days' time he had met and gotten hooked on another woman.

Amy said, "Some of my classmates are making much more than I am. And just yesterday my boss told me I was being transferred to another brand. He called it a promotion. But if I were doing a good job on the brand I have now, why would he take me off it? I don't even know if I can handle the new assignment. I'll probably fall on my face. In fact, they could be setting me up." "Have you tried to listen to your thoughts about yourself?" she was asked. "Do you know that your thoughts are doing destructive things to you?"

"Well, I can't help the way I *think*," was her immediate reaction. Her doctor assured her that someday she *could* be able to help the way she thought.

Amy was asked how she would feel if someone at work told her she was going to make a fool of herself. "Insulted!" she said.

"And what would you do if your best friend told you Don probably has someone else?" Without a moment's hesitation, Amy said, "I'd tell her just to cool it. What was she trying to do, making me feel worse?" "Exactly," the therapist responded. "And now you can get into the habit of 'cooling it' yourself."

This was a totally new concept to Amy. She had never compared her own voice to the voices of others.

The idea that she had been insulting herself, trying to make herself feel worse, was staggering to her. It was explained to her that her Inner Voice was in reality an amalgam of outside voices, many of them critical and pessimistic, many of them dating from early childhood. Without realizing it, she had assimilated them and was now playing them back in a steady stream to the detriment of her well-being. The actual repetition of those critical thoughts was the immediate cause of her depression.

At the end of her first visit, Amy was told to monitor her thoughts. She was asked to listen throughout the day—and particularly at night, if she was having trouble falling asleep. It would be even more helpful for her to jot down what she heard. Amy was skeptical at first that this would have any effect on the despair she was experiencing. But at her next appointment she confessed to being shocked by the relentless beating she was giving herself. She admitted, "In one day alone, I wrote down 26 negative thoughts. And I'm sure there were plenty I missed. No wonder I'm always tired and depressed." Her list included:

"I'm not really smart. I got ahead by a bunch of flukes."

"I'll never get that report done by the deadline."

"That meeting tomorrow will be a disaster. I never chaired a meeting before. Basically I'm a very shy person."

"Why is Don rejecting me? It's like I can have a relationship for seven months, and he gets the seven-month itch!"

"Nancy looks terrific today. I never look so put together."

"I wish that memo I wrote yesterday had been more tactful. Interpersonal stuff just is not my bag."

"My boss looked furious this morning. I wonder what I did."

"Uh-oh, Kathy wants to see me. What's bugging her now?"

"What will I do if Don never calls again?"

Her therapist then asked her to imagine someone close to her saying to her: "Amy, you're not smart." "Amy, you will never get that report done." "Amy, that meeting you're chairing tomorrow will be a disaster." "Amy, face it, you never do look as good as Nancy." "Amy, that was not a tactful memo you wrote. You just can't make it with people."

Amy began to grin in recognition. At the same time she was appalled at what she was doing to herself. Right there in the doctor's office she had become depressed about the terrible things being said to her. But then she began to get angry and stopped her therapist from going on and on down the list about how awful she was.

And then she realized that all these attacks on her were of her own making. She had never realized before that *that hurts just as much as if someone else put her down*. And she had the sense and the willpower to say "Stop" to her own thoughts.

That was Amy's introduction to Inner Speech Training.

Hearing that list read out loud, hearing her fears, doubts, and forebodings piled up like that—26 in one day, with more falling between the cracks—made her realize how much energy she was squandering on imagined catastrophes.

GETTING STARTED

Of course, Amy didn't turn her life around after two visits. She had a lot of work to do before she could conquer her self-critical, depressive thoughts and direct her Inner Voice into more powerful channels. What was important about those early visits is that she was able to see, for the first time, what her own thoughts were doing to *her*. She was putting the whammy on herself. That insight was the pivot on which her transformation turned.

Awareness is the crucial ingredient in any changes you want to make in yourself. And since your thoughts produce your feelings, it behooves you to be aware of your thoughts. Say you inexplicably felt anxious and uncomfortable all week. Nothing of consequence went wrong, yet the uneasiness is persistent. Since you can't shed the feeling, you console yourself by thinking, "It's something I can't control. Maybe it's all this rain we've been having. Dark days get everybody down." And so the gloomy feelings continue, slowing you down and taking the edge off life's small enjoyments.

But let's write another scenario. Suppose you sat down and probed systematically and got back to Tuesday morning when you overheard your boss say something about getting rid of the "dead wood." Immediately you thought, "That's me." *That thought* triggered your anxiety, and blocked further thought. If you had chosen to think further, you would have remembered that two staff members are due to retire and one keeps remarking, "This company is headed for Chapter Eleven, but it's no skin off my teeth."

Also, the new receptionist, a civic leader on his own time and on much of the office's, is on the phone to his state assemblyman more than he's taking incoming company calls.

There's dead wood to burn! You could have figured that out and saved yourself a week out of your life.

Can you change the way you think? With some practice you can, and that means you can also change your life. By focusing on your thinking, which is the cornerstone of your personality, you can achieve real personal growth. Again, Listen In to your thoughts as you read. Do you hear an internal voice repeating the words? That's what thinking is: silent, internal speaking. Do you also hear other words? Is your Inner Voice talking back as it absorbs the text, agreeing or disagreeing on some points, and elaborating on others with anecdotes of its own ("Like, what I tend to fall into...")?

This sort of thing goes on continually, and it influences both your moods and your responses to your environment. If you think of your mind in computer terms, you'll realize why data processors have the expression, "Garbage in, garbage out." What this means, simply, is that the result can't be better than the input. And the same principle applies to your mind.

To continue the analogy: *negative in, negative out*. Sometimes your mind seems programmed with put-down words as if your worst enemy were talking. (If you're that dangerous, you're actually pretty powerful.) When that occurs, the language of your inner speech will sabotage your confidence and satisfaction instead of offering support and encouragement.

As we'll see in the next chapter, your Inner Voice draws on many sources in the development of its incessant monologue. Since infancy, it has heard many voices saying many different things; yet it selects only certain of these to store in its memory. *All persons develop a particular style of thinking*, which in turn *determines their feelings and behavior*. Not everyone's inner speech is the same. Amy's was depressive; yours may be something quite different. But you can diagnose your own thinking and make it more effective. Once you're in control of your thoughts, you'll be able to eliminate many false moves.

You can remember when someone you admired said something very positive to you. Perhaps an upperclassman remarked that you had terrific energy. *"Energy?"* you thought, electrified. "You mean I'm not the lazy slob I always assumed?" That admired friend used cognitive restructuring on you. He or she said something that made you see yourself differently. And you became more secure and confident because that is the way that you then thought about yourself.

The shortcoming of many of those treasured accolades is that the inner speech that was implanted in your mind did not control your thinking for very long. All too soon, the habits of the years took over in your mind, and you were your old self—which meant that you hadn't restructured your thoughts permanently.

But for at least a brief time you had experienced that something transforming could happen to you by having a psychological "implant" in your brain—that is, the implant of some thoughts about you that were wonderfully positive. The person who complimented you gave you a new truth about yourself. The next chapter begins with the first technique that will help you implant some new truths about yourself—permanently.

When Amy came for therapy she would say: "I feel like I haven't really gotten anywhere. I feel like I missed the boat somehow." Amy began to make lasting progress in therapy when she learned the difference between her symptoms and her problem. Her symptoms were her discouraged feelings. She did not know what her problems were. She began to catch on when it was explained this way:

When you have a 103-degree fever, the fever is not the illness. A high fever is only a symptom of the illness—which may be, for example, an infection or a virus. The 103-degree fever is the effect. The infection is the cause. Amy's feelings were about as oppressive and disabling as a 103-degree fever; but they were not the cause. Those 103-degree feelings were the result of her problem.

She felt depressed, but that symptom was caused by her underlying problem which was: she thought she was a failure, she thought tomorrow would be a disaster, she thought she did not "have what it takes," that she had gotten by by faking it. Sometimes she thought she was going crazy.

After Amy understood that her recurrent thoughts were the real cause of her misery, she had a handle on her life, something that she could go to work on. It gave her a lift to know that she needed to work on her thoughts. She knew that here was something she could do.

THE CASE OF AMY 31

The one basic precept to keep in mind is: You are what you think. Remember also that you have the right and the wherewithal to direct your thinking into channels that work for you.

It's *your* mind.

CHAPTER 3

COGNITIVE RESTRUCTURING
CHANGING YOUR THINKING

Psychotherapy has come a long way since the days of endlessly probing into one's past and one's feelings. Not that either is to be discounted. Both our past and our feelings affect our actions. But people are thinking beings, and our thoughts exert a greater influence over our behavior. In the past decade, helping techniques have undergone a quiet but dramatic revolution. Treatment has become more effective and less time-consuming, with patients taking an active, rather than a passive, role in their own transformations.

Techniques come and go, but rarely does one produce results, in conjunction with more traditional therapies, as effectively as Cognitive Restructuring. The reason it seems to work is that it addresses the thinking human being we all know ourselves to be, and pride ourselves on being.

As important as it is to be in touch with our feelings, it is even more important to be *in touch with our thoughts*. Thoughts are often so entrenched we're not even conscious of their impact on us. Until we become aware of that Inner Voice, we may not know where our troubles come from: the weather, the family, the boss, our co-workers, our neighbors, any and all outside forces, whatever or whoever is handy. If these were the culprits, however, our lives would be hopeless because there isn't too much we can do about outside forces. Fortunately, though, we *can* change ourselves, and the truth is that at least 90 percent of our problems are self-generated by the thoughts we think. "The fault, dear Brutus, is not in our stars, but in ourselves—"

People who have Listened In on their minds at every opportunity have usually been aghast at what they've heard. Those who genuinely thought of themselves as victims of circumstance were suddenly introduced to an inner negative side of themselves they had never suspected was there.

They were the captive audience of inner speeches to themselves—inner speeches about themselves—that often predicted ruin and warned of danger. The result of those thoughts was that their thinkers felt frightened and helpless.

Cognitive restructuring—or "thought-changing" —teaches that you can be assertive in dealing with your own thoughts. It's *your* mind. So far, your mind may have had free rein. It's time to see what *you* can do— time to step in as director and take over. Since it *is* your mind, you have the right and the responsibility to decide what messages you want to receive. If the words you have been hearing attack you, demean you, or forecast failure and grief, they are saboteurs—in fact vandals—trashing your life, and you have the obligation to rout them. The mind is the domain of reason, but of *your* reason.

Once, years ago, we trained our minds so that

when we thought "nine times seven," we then thought 63. For a while we may have thought seven times eight was 63. As for the spelling of "weird," it's not "after *c*," and it's not "sounded like *a*," so who expects "*ei*"? Nevertheless we made the adjustment. Nine times seven being 63 and "weird" with *i after e* became second nature.

Most of us have some thinking patterns that make trouble for us—they may even program us to be anxious, frustrated, or to fail. Eventually, though, we can have habits of thinking that raise our spirits. We all know people who do it now. Few if any. Somehow they learned how to do it. You can learn to do it, too. If you change some of your thoughts, you can be more productive, and more fulfilled.

You can learn to instill habits of thinking which lift your spirits, and reduce depressing and anxious thoughts and feelings. You did it with arithmetic and spelling, and you can do it with your emotions—which are more important, and which you can't verify with a calculator or a dictionary.

The term Inner Speech Training is directly pictorial. "Inner" refers to your mental life. "Speech" means expressed in words. "Training" refers to a technique that can be learned. Nearly everyone has taken some form of training that worked. Relatively few people have been in therapy, and sometimes with uneven results. Since I.S.T. is available to all, the word "training" rather than therapy is used, although it is, of course, a form of therapy.

What is known about its effectiveness?

The National Institute of Mental Health, which is funded by the federal government, completed a $10 million study which was conducted over 6 years. The purpose of the study was, among others, to see if cognitive therapy for depression was as effective as drug treatment. The answer was a strong affirmative, and the results were publicized nationwide in the media.

It is on the principles of cognitive therapy that Inner Speech Training builds. Many of those methods have been refined in ways calculated to make them more quickly learned, more easily used, and better remembered. The next chapter describes how to begin to work at changing the distorted and destructive views of yourself that cause anxiety and depression. *Thinking that leads to depression is illogical.* Logic can be applied to such thinking in a way that lifts the depression.

The art of thinking is now being taught even in kindergartens. Many schools require courses in *how to think*, that is, how to find out how to solve problems and what causes what effect. Rather than just for memorizing facts, these new courses in thinking help students reflect upon whether or not an argument is logical, and whether the conclusions are supported by the facts.

Inner Speech Training builds on the research on thinking that is increasingly widespread in our general education system. Some psychology is mainly about thinking effectively about history or politics or literature. Here, the newest techniques of thinking are applied to your emotions and to your behavior. The research indicates that the more *actively* you process new learning, the better you retain it. If you will actively process your own thinking as you read, according to the methods set forth, you will be launched on the way to improving your mental health and well-being.

You can make your life miserable with what you

think, or you can change your thoughts and free your-self to make the most of life's experiences. Some people feel depressed when it rains. It is not the rain that causes their depression, but their *thoughts about* the rain. Others find a rainy day "nice and peaceful," or that "it makes the house so cozy." Any art student can tell you that it is an overcast landscape, not a sunny one, that shows its colors most intensely. It's on a "gray day" that the grass is actually *greenest.*

You can dwell on all the things that are "getting worse": the traffic, the mails, the neighborhood, and, of course, "the *service.*" Your thoughts won't get the bank to hire more tellers, won't erase graffiti, or alter other drivers' manners. But you can decide to stop your inner emotional irritation by changing what you are thinking about. You can monitor what is called your "useless worry" and use your 13 billion brain cells for subjects far more diverting.

Inner Speech Training will not make you a mind-less Pollyanna, which is not the idea. But a number of studies have discovered that choosing to think opti-mistically will actually bring about a more successful outcome.

Self-fulfilling prophecies do tend to produce the re-sults they predict. The research shows that if you can prophesy in your inner speech that you will do well in a test, or prophesy as you prepare for a dinner party that your guests will have a good time, you will be in much better form for the test and for the dinner party. You can give your thoughts the power to improve your be-havior. Pessimistic thinking, on the other hand, saps your mental energy and slows down your responses.

You may have grown up in a home where you were taught to expect the worst. That is a set of thoughts that *has been proved to produce depression.* Since that style of thinking was *learned, it can be unlearned.*

You probably want to change at least some of your self-talk. Here is how to get started.

CHAPTER 4

INNER SPEECH TECHNIQUE #1:
LISTENING IN
LOCATING YOUR INNER VOICE

The first basic step in Inner Speech Training is

POWER THINKING TECHNIQUE #1: LISTENING IN
Listening In is training to hear yourself thinking.

Thinking is *Inner Speech*.

Thoughts require words which unite to form dialogues internally as inner speech *to ourselves* — or *between* ourselves and *someone else*.

To "Listen In" to the dialogues in your head, train yourself to become more aware of exactly what your thoughts are telling you at any given moment.

The first basic idea of Cognitive Therapy is that the thinking we do — the very thoughts we think — influences our feelings and behavior. The second is that by monitoring our thinking, we can change it. Once we do that, we will automatically have gained *power over our feelings and behavior*, and as soon as we start to use that power, our lives take on a new brightness.

43

How do you train yourself to hear the voices of your inner speech?

This is a *real* voice we're talking about, not an imaginary one. It rules you with its choice of words. The unhealthy voices have a tendency to use the same words again and again. They specialize in imperatives, put-downs, doubts, and regrets. Over and over, you're getting messages like, "You've got to..." "You'll never..." "I wish..." "See what you went and did?," and these messages undermine you. Once you're tuned into your Inner Voice, you're on your way to taking charge. You'll be able to make your thoughts do your bidding, rather than the other way around. And once that happens, your feelings and actions will change, too.

1. Identify *who* is doing the speaking.
2. Identify *what* actual words are used.
3. Identify the *tone* of voice. Is it critical carping, judgmental?
4. What *feelings* are triggered by the word-thoughts in your head? Do your feelings show the words to be guilt-producing—and outdated, inappropriate ones?

Why don't you?	Why can't you?
When I was your age...	Why haven't you?
	You'd better be!
You should do that.	You must be punctual
You should be!	to be successful.

These are examples of how our Inner Voices interfere with our conscious intentions. Multiply them a thousandfold, and you'll see to what extent you're being diverted from your positive goals. Unless you listen carefully to your thoughts, they control you and cause you to *act against yourself*. By not answering that insidious Inner Voice, you allow it to continue dominating your mind.

A CASE OF SIMPLE CONFUSION

Consider the case of the well-meaning young married woman who kept confusing herself. In her head, she thought she heard: "I love my husband, Steve, so much." Yet she felt anger and even resentment at her husband constantly for his staying out late at night.

When she worked at it and learned to Listen In accurately she could hear the actual voice in her head, which turned out to be: "I'm being taken advantage of. I *hate* it." No wonder she was confused without being able to be aware and listen in to her thinking.

Remember that it is important *actually* to hear the "exact" words so that you can then account for the distortion in your feelings.

Listening In can be used in a variety of circumstances. For example, consider the thoughts connected with feelings such as

Regret. "What should I have done?"

Mind racing (anticipation). "What will I do if..."

Performance anxiety. "How will I ever get done on time?"

Depression (universalizations and generalizations). "Nothing ever goes right for me."

Obsession. "Did I remember to turn off the gas?"

WHERE DO YOU THINK?

You have an Inner Speech Center where your thinking actually occurs. Practice locating your inner voice center.

Place your index finger as far into your mouth as you can reach and touch the top part of your mouth (your upper palate). Your inner voice is *usually centered* just above and a little behind this point. If you close your eyes and listen carefully, it probably feels as if it is almost behind your eyes and midway between your ears. Some people locate it a bit differently, at the base of the skull.

Listen In carefully as you read and think the words in front of your eyes. Can you vividly feel the spot in your head where your inner speech is located? You are hearing an *Internalization* of your own voice. Say the words "inner voice" to yourself. Did you feel and hear where you said it?

Right now, you are experiencing the words before you. This very moment you are having the sense of the words being repeated in your mind as you read: This is what thinking is.

Train yourself to experience the sensation of thinking as you think about some other thoughts.

Picture yourself at an intersection.

"Which road shall I take?"

Listen In. Could you hear the inner dialogue and word-thoughts that come as a response to that question located by the same control part of your head?

Thinking is to speak silently, internally, with an inner

voice. Your inner voices are not permanent. If you teach yourself to Listen In to your thoughts, you can train yourself, and in time, change yourself.

In fact, *all psychotherapy is training yourself to think better.* It provides a system to approach one's own mind. You can use your brain to work on your brain. Unmonitored and unexamined inner speech can lead you to become your own worst enemy. Fortunately, human beings are unique in their capacity for self-improvement and change.

Have you ever—

Caught yourself thinking about something else while you are making love so that you couldn't really enjoy lovemaking?

Worried so much about an examination that you couldn't study?

Experienced mind-racing which occurs when thoughts are going so fast that you can't fall asleep because your mind is too busy—trying to undo your past—or planning your future, trying to resolve yet unborn problems?

If you have done these things, you need to practice *Listening In* as the first step, the first building block in your new thinking system.

We all know people like Fran S., the woman whose critical internal voice said,

"I'm only a secretary."

If she had Listened In to her own inner speech, she would have heard the weakening of her personality and self-confidence conveyed in the use of the word "only."

THE STORY OF LINDA

To illustrate why tuning in to your thoughts is so important, there is the extreme case of an intelligent young woman who had cut herself off from her Inner Voice until it was nearly too late. Rather than getting in touch with the source of her problem, Linda had been distracting herself with food. As soon as she felt tense, she'd eat something, and that would help her relax. Once she bought herself a cheesecake and a spoon, and ate it, undefrosted, in her parked car. She felt she should lose 10 or 15 pounds, but had not been able to do it, even though she had tried three expensive diet programs — one, costing $200, limiting her menu to three vitamin beverages a day.

When Linda began Inner Speech Training to work on her weight and her depression, she was asked what was troubling her. She replied that she was lonely and frightened. Frightened of what? She wasn't sure — just a general feeling of fear that seemed to be with her all the time. Therapy began with the detective work of uncovering the causes of her fears.

Linda was given an assignment to work on between sessions: "Jot down the thought that comes to mind each time you think of having something to eat. Your thought may not always be complete, but even a word or two will help. Also, jot down any thought you had just before your mood dropped."

During the next few sessions, Linda made progress in sketching her background. Her father had always been a drinker, given to the classic behavior patterns of the alcoholic. His moods were unpredictable and extreme, alternating between angry outbursts and tenderness and sentimentality. In his wilder moments, he would swear at his three children and frighten them with threats of beating. At other times, he would reverse himself, accuse them of avoiding him, and lavish caresses on them.

It made for an insecure, tense environment. Linda was a good student, popular with girlfriends, but she avoided boys. As soon as she had her high school diploma in hand, she left home for New York City. She started college part-time and got a good job as a hostess in a high-class restaurant. She was tall, slim, attractive, and had a pleasant smile. She looked sophisticated and handled both the job and her college schedule well.

Men seemed to like Linda. They often complimented her, and in the restaurant, she was conscious of their eyes on her. From time to time, customers asked her out, and occasionally she went, but she never dated anyone more than once or twice. "Between school and work, I was too busy for a social life," she said.

After a few months, Linda had found herself struggling to get ready to go to work every evening. She had no idea why. She felt a vague uneasiness when she was at the restaurant. A sense of discomfort accompanied her every time she walked across the room to seat a guest, and it seemed even more oppressive when she walked back to her station alone. But, somehow she found no link between her disquiet and the admiring stares.

She began staying behind the little reservation desk as much as possible, as if hiding. She began to perspire when she had to go into the bar. She soon found she could breathe more easily out in the kitchen, and she began to make excuses to go there. She'd nibble on something and immediately feel more relaxed.

"Oh," she thought, "I'll take a bowl of peanuts from the bar and keep it handy at the reservation stand." The peanuts led to bread sticks and rolls; the bread, to desserts; the desserts, to chocolate bars in her purse. Soon she couldn't leave for work without having a bite to eat, in spite of the fact that her job included dinner. Naturally enough, she gained weight.

As Linda told her story, she was asked occasionally about what she was thinking, and to check on whether she was listening to herself as she talked. Little by little, she learned the habit of hearing what she was saying. Finally, she made a breakthrough. She was talking about her father, saying that he wasn't really so bad — "He really loved us" — when she started to cry. She said, "He was a shit. He was Dad, so we loved him, but he was a shit." Here at last was her honest Inner Speech about her father (and men).

She had started to overeat when her job required her to be in contact with men, and what was worse for her, when she was required to be pleasant and friendly to them. Food worked for Linda like a tranquilizer. She could smother her thoughts with food. When she discovered that her problems were based on her disgust and fear of men, she learned to Listen In to those thoughts and deal with them directly. She soon was able to catch the thought that disturbed her, before she turned to thoughts of food. The dieting was still not easy, and her depression hung on for some time, but now she knew *where to attack* her misery. Her time was better spent working on her thoughts and fears of men, rather than trying to avoid calories.

Like Linda, most people are not always aware of what their inner voice is saying. Linda found that Inner Speech Training helped her to "think out" her problems rather than "act out." When she could face the thought about her mistrust of men, she did not need to resort to food in order to tranquilize her fearful, but largely subconscious, thought. Linda had begun to have trouble with her weight at the same time that she began to be seriously attracted to men. Her inner speech problem was that she had contradictory voices trying to occupy her mind at the same time. She liked men and she distrusted them, and she began to overeat to stop the inner tension she felt.

Do you ever feel divided in your thinking? Is there a sense that your thoughts are dominated by dissenting factions? The pros and cons are filibustering in your head.

"This new job has a future."	"But fifteen years with a company, you just don't walk away from."
"If I accept this date, we might hit it off and have a great time."	"If he gets pushy because he thinks he's supposed to, it'll just be so embarrassing."

With debates like these spinning their wheels, of course you're never going to get anywhere.

LEARNING HOW YOU THINK

Before you can fix something, you need to know how it works, which is why *Listening In* is Step 1 of the I.S.T. program. It starts when you make a conscious effort to hear the words that are churning inside your head. Repeat them out loud if that will help you capture them, even tape them. Jot them down if you have a chance. But whatever you do, be as *precise* as you can. The most helpful clues are the actual words themselves.

Whenever you have just had a change in your mood, *a thought preceded* and *caused* that mood change. If your mood lightened so that you felt more upbeat, you had an optimistic, pleasant or (for you) a rewarding thought. The new thought may have been something as simple as *Listening In* to a one-liner in a show you watched, or overheard in a store.

If you find that your mood dropped and you became gloomy, it was caused by your thought of being overwhelmed by something—anything from breaking your shoelace when you were in a rush, to thinking about how you were going to pay for your children's college.

You will learn better how to influence your feelings, and ultimately your whole life, when you become a master at *connecting* your *mood* changes *with the thought* that caused the dip or upswing. When you know the cause of your feelings, you can change them.

After you've had some practice, *Listening In* will become increasingly automatic. As you're walking along the street or driving in your car or sitting in someone's waiting room, you can actually be intrigued by your inner speech. You can tune in to your silent broadcast. Think of it as an educational program sponsored by yourself for yourself.

You will find it instructive to identify the substance of what you're hearing. Is it critical? Contradictory? Discouraging? Take a few minutes to analyze your messages, and then see how they make you feel. Are they guilt-producing? Do you hear your parents so often that you feel like a child again—in which case, how can you possibly lead an adult's life, even a very simple one? Do you feel harassed by "don'ts" and "shoulds" and endless streams of commands? "Don't interrupt." "Don't get in over your head." "You should always listen." "Don't be foolhardy." "Make the most of any opportunity." "Being a maverick will get you nowhere." "Staying with the herd you'll never get ahead." "Get a haircut." "Remember, the first thing people see is your fingernails."

Too many of us tolerate critical and demeaning voices in our minds, to prove that we "can take criticism." These self-critical thoughts can lead to a disabling loss of self-esteem. *Listen In, and you can change!*

SUMMING UP

Listening In is Technique #1 of I.S.T. It involves getting in touch with your Inner Voice, a process that will lead to astonishing disclosures. *Listening In* will intensify your awareness of what is going on in your head, and it will start you off on the program that can make the rest of your life easier and more gratifying.

CHAPTER 5

INNER SPEECH TECHNIQUE #2: UNDERLINING
LOCATING YOUR DESTRUCTIVE VOICE

Underlining, the second major technique for under-standing and changing your thinking, builds on Tech-nique #1—*Listening In*.

POWER THINKING TECHNIQUE #2: UNDERLINING

Underlining means selecting the specific words in your internal dialogue that are destructive to you. As you *Listen In* to your word thoughts, some words will soon stand out as culprits. *Underline* them so that they become obvious to you. Once you have Underlined the words, you can act to change them constructively.

Have you ever tried to break a bad habit? Cutting down on coffee, for example. You may get through the first day without too much effort, but the minute the stress piles up, you reach for a cup. That is, unless you're very alert.

It's the same with your thoughts. They are habits

and they are persistent. You will need a *plan*, so that your habitual thoughts don't prevail. Now that you have heard what's going on in your head and realize that at times your Inner Voice is more negative than is doing you any good, recall the words of Thomas Mann: "Self-Examination, if it is thorough enough, is nearly always the first step toward change."

Perhaps you noticed a kind of sameness when you practiced *Listening In*. Perhaps certain words and phrases cropped up more often than you had expected. Think back. Did some thoughts have a familiar ring, like an old song—not necessarily a goldie—that gets stuck in your head and haunts you all day long? If they did, those are the thoughts to be on the lookout for. They're the ones that probably are sabotaging you. They have to be watched. Many of us tend to be careless with our thinking, allowing it to "just happen." It usually "just happens" to fall into repetitive patterns.

Think of all the people you know whose speech is peppered with verbal tics, who can't get through a sentence without "I mean," "Know what I'm saying?" "Right?" or some other jab-in-the-ribs phrase. And the ones who preface every anecdote with "Listen to this" or "You'll never believe..."?

Much the same is true of our Inner Voices. Over the years, they have developed a particular style, and more often than not, those stock phrases are damaging. Like Fran S.'s Inner Voice that kept telling her that she was "only a secretary," Mark's kept telling him that he was "just a salesman." With the seemingly unimportant word "only," or "just," both of them were not only downgrading their job, but by extension, themselves. Fran S. and Mark were both victims of their own Inner Voice.

For Mark, *Listening In* was a revelation, and when he moved on to *Underlining*, he began to make progress. *Underlining* helped him highlight his Inner Speech errors. For the first time, he caught vivid glimpses of what his Inner Voice was doing to him.

Underlining builds very closely on *Listening In*. When you practiced listening, you became aware of what your Inner Speech was like. Now, with *Underlining*, you'll be highlighting the deadly words and phrases that poison your thoughts. The positive parts of your thinking, the thoughts that bolster you, don't need any attention. They're doing their job. What you need to concentrate on are the messages you don't need to hear.

WHEN TO USE UNDERLINING

Underlining can be particularly effective if you have a tendency to make *premature judgments* either *about yourself* or other people.

"I always feel dumb at parties."   "I'll never pick up an instrument, I don't have an ear."

Or if you are troubled by *painful recurring* thoughts...

"Why can't he feel about me like I do about him?"

Or if you can't handle relationships and they get out of control. First your thoughts *set you up* and then *put you down*.

"I don't have any trouble *getting* someone—
it's hanging *onto* them. It shows something's
lacking in me."

By *Underlining* the negative word or phrase, you can
easily see the damage you do to yourself.

The following dialogues show how to Underline
the culprit. Watch for the anxiety-creating and
depression-producing words.

Listen In and Underline the damaging thoughts in
this inner dialogue.

INNER DIALOGUE #1

"I'm a *lousy* swimmer (tennis player, golfer,
lover, cook, carpenter, conversationalist,
etc.)."

Comment: The "damaging" word to Underline
here is "lousy." All this statement does is make you feel
hopeless. It is *useless self-criticism*. Why is it necessary
to judge yourself that way? Is it possible that you enjoy
splashing around in the water even though you can't
swim well?

Your thoughts may be stimulated by what is happening in the *present* but their destructive powers *origi-
nate* out of *habits* built in the most impressionable years,
the period of early life. In emotionally charged situations, the tendency is very strong to draw on and repeat
the old automatic thoughts without stopping to examine and explore more effective alternatives. These old
destructive word-thoughts will continue automatically
unless they are underlined.

For instance, do you hear:

External (Someone remarks to you):	*Your translation* (As heard in your voice thoughts):
"What are you doing here?"	"He's not happy to see me."
"I was going to call you."	"But you thought better of it."
"How are you holding up in this heat?"	"I look pretty scuzzy."

These are defects in the way that you perceive and relate to your world. If your own thinking is set up to discredit you, you are speaking internally to yourself in ways that produce the two major factors in neurosis: anxiety and depression.

This is a critical area. You may be misinterpreting how others see you. You may be using an inner language, or system of inner dialogues, that leads to feeling weak or immature, because your inner thoughts distort what others mean by what they say.

Ask yourself if your internal language is a positive one. Do you cause things to go well for you? Or is your language a negative one? Are the negative voices limited to certain areas like sex or relationships with peers or authority persons? Are you distorting the same things over and over in your mind? Hardly anyone uses enough power in his or her thinking.

The choice of the words in your inner speech makes the difference between success or failure, between mental health and neurosis.

The boss said, "You're looking good." You heard in your mind, "I don't look as fat."

Is your inner speech a wrong interpretation that leads to disturbing feelings?

You can *disconnect* the external remark from the faulty translation. You can do this by hearing the *exact words* of the other person. "You're looking good." *Do not add any other words.*

INNER DIALOGUE #2

Listen In and Underline the weak word.

"I'll never get out of sex what people are supposed to. I'm just not any good at making love."

Comment: Underline *Never.* "Never" is used here to deny responsibility for your sexuality, and promote failure. What about enjoying *love?* Keep score of your self-criticisms. Count the number of times you criticize yourself in an hour. Who gets punished beside yourself?

INNER DIALOGUE #3

Weak Thinking:

"Why did I pig out on that birthday cake? I'll always be a blimp."

Comment: Underline *"always be a blimp."* Don't weaken yourself further by thinking in *self-critical* terms that prevent you from reaching your goal.

INNER DIALOGUE #4

Weak Thinking:

"Nothing I do *ever* seems to come out *right."*

Comment: Underline 2½ damaging words. "Nothing" and "ever" definitely serve to deplete the thinker. Also, the word "right" often defeats a person. This is a perfect example of *depressogenic* thinking—which actually generates depression. It can make you depressed because it overgeneralizes, and sabotages your basic good feelings about yourself.

INNER DIALOGUE #5

Weak Thinking: How many times have you heard in your own mind, or in someone else's speech:

"If only I would meet the right person, then *nothing else would really matter."*

Comment: Underline the two weak phrases *"if only"* and *"nothing else would really matter."* That kind of thinking condemns you to procrastination and lack of action. If you keep waiting for a magical solution that is going to take care of everything, your thoughts will grind your life to a halt.

You can practice by *Listening In,* and listing the most common ways you criticize yourself.

1. "I always have problems with figures..." (The use of *"always"* condemns you.)

(Try filling in the next two examples.)
2. I...
3. I...

While you are *Listening In*, try to isolate and Underline the weakening words or phrases.

Finally, try to notice *who* is doing the criticism in your internal voices. Is it your own voice, or is someone else controlling your thinking? What is the tone of voice used?

It is important at this point to decide whether the invading voices are supportive and friendly, or contemptuous, harsh, and hostile. Once you determine these characteristics, and to whom the voice belongs, you can more easily decide whether the voice is saying anything real or whether it should be blotted out.

INNER DIALOGUE #6

Weak Thinking:

"Nothing I do makes any sense."

Combine the first two power thinking techniques now:

Listen In: "Nothing I do makes any sense."

Underline: "*Nothing* I do makes *any* sense." Say it slowly. Brake it: Nothing—I—do—makes—any—sense. Can you hear the damaging words you are saying to yourself?

Braking here slows down the speed of your thoughts and allows you to have a better sense of where the word-thoughts are leading. It is a helpful part of *Listening In* and *Underlining*. You can consciously put the brake on your speeding thoughts.

Slow — down — the — words — in — each — sentence — in — your — head. Listen in to each word and replay it at low speed. Take—it—easy. Train yourself to relax by applying the brakes to your internal dialogue.

Psychotherapy sessions often include *Underlining* and *Braking* in order to help a patient hear the self-defeating statement he or she just made. When the words are slowed down enough so they can be heard more clearly, the patient can stop the "mindless" repetitive self-putdowns.

These techniques are vital to gaining control over unwanted thoughts and fears. There is a real "inner self" in a person which can evaluate the absurdity of obsessional and phobic thoughts—once those thoughts are pinpointed through *Listening In* and *Underlining*.

When you Underline a damaging word, you don't actually have to write the words down and draw a line underneath them. But if you can, it helps. The more you stress the destructive words and bring them into the open, the more power you have over them. Once they're written down, you can confront them in black-and-white. They cease to be fleeting, hit-and-run type missiles that wing you and take off. You can look at them several times during the day and memorize them.

Saying them out loud is also effective, especially if you repeat them a few times. If you're in a situation where you don't want to be seen talking to yourself, repeat them silently.

Those seemingly innocuous, but actually harmful words have gone unnoticed too long. What has made them so powerful until now was their ability to escape exposure, to strike when you weren't paying attention,

or your resistance was low. Once you have isolated
them and brought them out of hiding, the odds change
in your favor. You'll be able to change those hurtful
words to more constructive ones.

For Fran S. and Mark, the culprit was "only," or
"just." Once that negative word is eliminated from the
message, there's nothing weakening about thinking or
saying "I'm a salesman," or "I'm a secretary." On the
contrary, both statements hold possibilities. They open
the door to many positive follow-ups, such as "I make a
bundle, when you figure fringes," or "I'm on my way
up the ladder."

Most of us have too many words like "only" in our
thoughts. "Never" is one of the most common culprits.

THE EXPERIENCE OF NORA

Nora came to therapy in a state of shock that her
boyfriend had called her "basically cold." "Our sex life's
the greatest," she insisted. "If anything, I'm more
horny than he is, but I know not to make a bunch of
demands."

In fact, it turned out Nora "knew not to" show
much of any feelings at all. It was a family code. "Never
show blood to the enemy," her father had told her. Her
mother said, "Never let on to a man he means anything
to you. Right then he loses interest."

Nora had lived with her boyfriend for three years,
they had joint bank accounts and discussed marriage
and children, but true to the principle of "Never show
weakness," she had never told him she loved him. Yet it
seemed that the omission itself handed him a weapon.
When they broke up he said, "You never said you loved

me." "You see?" said her father. "Men never know what they want." "He should know," said her mother. "You did right. You never put yourself on the line." Nora's "never" family was vindicated indeed. Asked if she *did* love her boyfriend, Nora said, "I never really thought about it." In a reserved voice, as if queried on a sexual technicality, she explained, "I never really deal in terms of that."

Our first relationships were formed with our parents. To at least some extent, what happened between us and them serves as a model for all our subsequent relationships. It's not our purpose here to delve into those interactions, nor to turn parents as a group into scapegoats. To be pointed out, however, is that parents have the singular job of civilizing us—of teaching to discriminate right from wrong, of passing along social skills, of protecting us from danger. And some parents, however well-meaning they were, left us with fears and guilts that do not help us at all as adults. "Never cross against the lights" won't protect us from the turning cars, and "Never let anybody be too sure of you" is no protection against loss.

If your parents were overzealous about their responsibilities, or if they were weighted down with more than their share of their own fears and inhibitions, you may have been overwhelmed with injunctions.

Few of us have to think long to recall some of those "shoulds," "shouldn'ts," "oughts," and "musts." "You should have tried harder." "You shouldn't have stayed out so late." "You ought to be glad you have a new brother." "You either clean up your mess or I'm throwing it all out." All those precepts live on inside of us. We can overhaul and streamline lives by discarding the ones that do not apply to us now. If your *Underlining* technique is always handy, you will learn to pick up on the words and phrases that hurt you now.

Your most tenacious habits were formed in your most impressionable years—the years of early life. As you were learning to speak, your Inner Voice was learning right along with you. It has had many years to build up a stockpile of messages that condition you and cause you to do their bidding. Under emotionally charged situations, the tendency is even stronger to draw on these old accustomed responses without stopping to examine and explore more effective and appropriate alternatives. Unless your word-thoughts are interrupted, they're virtually automatic.

Underlining will put you into touch with your own weak thoughts. Suppose you're *Listening In* and you hear your Inner Voice state, "I'm hopeless at math." Immediately underline "hopeless." That term (the inner words in your mind) makes you feel exactly that. It certainly serves no positive purpose. To whom are you comparing yourself, Goedel?

Your thinking has just discredited you. You have been victimized by your own putdown. A damaging area, this. In the putdown, your Inner Voice sent you subtle, failure-provoking messages that caused you to feel weak or immature. Be on the lookout for them. Underline them. Just the existence of that thought in your mind, "hopeless," causes you to feel less of a person. It may seem too simple a technique to you right now; but if you *do not think that thought,* you will feel more effectual. Here is a challenge:

You can become a winner in the contest with your thoughts. You have now two valuable techniques that build on each other to help you. As you train yourself to use them, they'll become increasingly effective, and you'll find yourself gaining confidence in situations that used to throw you. Follow these Inner Speech Training pointers:

1. Review the procedures for *Listening In*.
2. Add *Underlining*.
3. Identify the weakening words you hear in your thoughts.
4. Repeat them. Write them down or say them out loud if you can. If not, say them silently.
5. Disconnect other people's words from the words your Inner Voice is saying.
6. Brake your damaging thoughts. Slow — them — down — so — you — can — really — hear — them. Those "never" sentences often have one plus; they're good for a laugh, and not on you.

CHAPTER 6

INNER SPEECH TECHNIQUE #3:
STOPPING
ENDING NEGATIVE THINKING

TECHNIQUE #3: STOPPING

Stopping occurs after you become aware of a particular thought by *Listening In* and using *Underlining* to decide that the thought is undesirable and needs to be stopped. The technique itself involves producing a word—"STOP"—in your internal thinking. Whenever the undesirable thought or thoughts occur you give the command, STOP!

Stopping is a definite technique in which you extinguish the weakening thought. Each time, Stop.
"What will I do if...?" STOP
"What will I do...?" STOP
Interrupt each time at an earlier and earlier point. Train yourself to interrupt your inner speech earlier.
"What will I...?" STOP
"What will...?" STOP
"What...?" STOP
STOP

73

That makes sense...But...But what do I do when I'm panicked?

The first thing you do is to STOP the inner voice...the speech that ignited and triggered the panic.

To demonstrate the importance of *Stopping*, we'd like to tell you about two men—Paul and Harvey— whose harmful thinking followed a remarkably similar course. Both of them were in their thirties, had good jobs, devoted wives, and adorable children. In both cases, the trouble started when their jobs required them to fly out of state once a week. Both Paul and Harvey were afraid of flying. Neither of them could get on a plane without hearing the alarm go off: "What if we crash?"

Both men were logical and well-informed. On a rational level, they knew that flying was safer than driving a car. But their Inner Voices were insistent. As each trip approached, the same message began banging away, "Suppose we crash.."

Paul and Harvey (who didn't know each other) both saw this phobia ruining their lives. They both decided to try therapy. Paul went into conventional psychotherapy. In the course of his treatment he came to understand that his fear was due to an early separation anxiety. He learned a lot about himself and his fears. He and his therapist were sure that in due time, he would work out his anxieties, including the phobia about flying. But by then, he might have been shoved aside in favor of an employee who always had his under-the-seater packed for Rio, Tokyo, and you name it.

Harvey, on the other hand, had heard about Inner Speech Therapy from a friend. His first appointment happened to be on the day following a trip. As he told his story, he broke out into a sweat. The mere mention of a plane was enough to set him off. But he began to work immediately on his phobia. Painstakingly he concentrated on identifying those "what ifs" and "supposes." He isolated his tendency to catastrophize. He went through I.S.T. step by step. Before many days had passed, Harvey learned to confront that Inner Voice of his and deal with it directly. He traced the source of his messages to a particularly fear-ridden housekeeper who had had charge of him when he was a child. He paid close attention to the weakening words—those fear-filled thoughts he had been taught to think when he was small. And he heard a variation of those thoughts when he boarded a plane.

As he moved on to the technique of *Stopping*, and mastered it, he had increasing success. To his amazement, he found himself able to *cut off* the voices that petrified him; slowly at first, but more rapidly as he practiced. From *Stopping*, he went on to the next step, *Switching*, where he learned to substitute more positive, fortifying thoughts, coupled with relaxation techniques—more about which in the next chapters. For now, it's important to know that it took Harvey only a small fraction of the time (and money) that Paul spent before he was able to fly without a panic attack.

When time is of the essence, I.S.T. gets to the heart of the matter—namely, a defect in your thinking—with dispatch. And it allows you to act against what is causing you to be afraid.

"What will I do if the plane crashes?" This is a worthless thought. It leads to phobias; it touches off a ridiculous type of worry about a situation over which you have no control. This thought has served to wreck more vacations than rain. You want to STOP such thinking. How to do it is to *STOP!*

In theory, *Stopping* is a very simple technique. In practice, it's not as easy as it sounds. All it requires is to produce one short word—STOP—every time you hear a weakening word in your head: that's all. To be effective at *Stopping*, you want to be forceful, assertive, tenacious. This is no time for a dialogue. Those damaging thoughts must be crushed as soon as they begin. *Stopping* takes determination—and a lot of practice.

Vera, who had been suffering from a chronic depression for years, was enthusiastic about Inner Speech Therapy and couldn't understand why it wasn't working for her. She was a musician and inclined to be introverted. Very diligent and sensitive, as a child she had been subjected to the strictest discipline: hours of practice on the cello; high standards for school work; punishment for the slightest infraction; no excuses allowed; no talking back.

When she demonstrated to her therapist how she practiced *Stopping*, it became clear why Vera wasn't getting any results. Her "Stop" came out in a whisper. It was so halting and almost pleading that her thoughts went sailing over it without the least hesitation. It took time, but eventually Vera learned to assert herself— even to bark "Stop" like a drill sergeant to help her release her inhibitions and to learn that it was permissible to be tough.

"Tough" is the operative word here. If, like Vera, you've never been tough before, train yourself. Raise your voice. And when you give a command, make it a monologue. Don't let those weakening words have a chance. It's your show. Picture yourself drowning out the inner voice of fear. It's your own mind. You are entitled to quash and rout invaders.

Here we come to a paradox. At the same time that you're being relentless with your negative thoughts, you want to be kind to yourself. Always keep in mind whose side you're on. *You* are not the enemy. The enemy is the negative thoughts. You don't want to add to your distress. Remember: You're on *your* side. Although you have to be harsh with the unpleasant *thought*, to Stop it, you don't extend the harshness to *yourself*. Here are some "Don'ts" to keep in mind:

> Don't say things to yourself like, "Stop it, stupid." Name-calling is no way to treat the person who means the most to you.
> Don't harp on your lapses (no "There you go again" or "Why can't you learn?")
> Don't be judgmental.

No one who has ever waked up with the kind of thoughts that come before it gets light will say that it is easy to Stop and Switch. Those thoughts of people you won't be seeing again, of unfulfilled ambitions, of a raft of unfinished and seemingly impossible chores, and a twinge in an infected hangnail bound to be gangrenous by morning are sometimes called the 4 a.m. "crazies." Crazy, because everyone is "crazy" when asleep, and therefore perhaps half-crazy when half-asleep. At 4 a.m. the body is at its lowest ebb, blood sugar and energy down, not having been fed since dinner the night before. Depression is partly physical and partly mental.

At these rock-bottom hours, *kindness toward yourself* is your best strategy. In those darkest periods, you most need the Stop and Switch techniques, but that is when they seem most impossible to use. Practicing without demanding perfection of yourself at 4 a.m. will eventually help you gain better control of your thoughts. No one is perfect. Mistakes are a fact of life, and that's the way it is. But you can hold the hope that your use of I.S.T. will make you much stronger in your thinking than before you began to use it. You'll get far more desirable results by being sympathetic to yourself and lenient toward your efforts.

A good way to follow up your STOP command is to say something like, "You're dwelling on old regrets." "Your thoughts are filled with useless recriminations." "Your Inner Voice is making you feel depressed." "The kind of thinking you're doing is panicking you."

Another good idea is to ask yourself, "*Why* am I doing this to myself?" "Is it helpful?" "Is it making me feel better?" "Is it cost-effective?" "Do these thoughts solve any of my problems—past, present, or future?" If the answer is "no," STOP. STOP. STOP. Don't victimize yourself.

How to Apply Stopping

In its straightforward way, *Stopping* is a high-powered technique for extinguishing your weakening thoughts. Whenever an undesirable message comes through, give the command, STOP. Try to block the thought as *early* as you can. Nip it in the bud. The forceful manner we described above will help. If possible, keep the thought from finishing itself. This will take some practice, but don't get discouraged. As you persevere, you'll become more adept at the technique, just as runners or swimmers or violinists do at the techniques they're trying to perfect.

Some thoughts will yield themselves to the technique of Stopping more readily than others. You may have an instant triumph with a chance thought like, "Jerk that I am, I forgot to turn off the radio." If that kind of thought is not part of your habitual thinking, it will respond at once to your STOP command. And it should be stopped. There are better ways to talk to yourself about an oversight.

Where you'll have more difficulty is with the thoughts that *are* habitual: the ones your Inner Voice sends forth with regularity. The put-downs that make you feel worthless. The constant harping on a particular subject: "I'll never win any popularity contest. I could count my friends on one hand and include slight acquaintances." Comparisons with others! "I'm two years older than Pete, and he's rich." "I'm not a barrel of laughs like Beth—I'm a heavy." Wish fantasies: "If Dreamboat Brad from back in school would call me up and say, 'All these years I've never been able to get you out of my mind.' "

We all have some category of thinking that is our own private patented brand of negativity. These thoughts are the persistent ones. As you probably learned when you practiced Listening In, they recur interminably. They'll do their best to defeat you, to slip past your STOP commands, to reappear when you're off guard. You may have to turn them off 20 or 30 times a day. But keep at it. *These* are the *really* destructive thoughts, the ones that sap your energy, deprive you of good feelings, throw you into a panic, and destroy your self-confidence. Those habitual painful thoughts are probably criticisms or teasings that you heard a thousand times as a child. "Call her anything but late for dinner." "Foot in your mouth." "Two left feet." What do you still hear from your childhood?

For these persistent messages, *Stopping* is more effective when it's done out loud. Whenever you can, let yourself *hear* that word, STOP. It reinforces the process and makes you stronger next time. Another helpful device is keeping track of how many times a day you're confronted by a particular thought. You'll get a lot of encouragement from seeing the number of repetitions dwindle as you become more skilled at *Stopping*.

WORRYING

Worry seems to be a basic fact of life. No one escapes it entirely, but some of us make a career of it. For the really accomplished worrier, who worries day and night about things that may or may not happen, everything is grist for the mill. Burglars. Accidents. Failures. What other people will think. What the weather will be tomorrow. We even know someone who worries because he read that the sun has only 2 billion years of life left.

There's no sense in worrying about things you can't help: That the Polar ice cap is melting and its flood is heading for New York, particularly East 20th Street. But we all have worries that are equally fruitless. A divorced mother has let four-year-old Garth visit his father, counting on her ex's girlfriend to look after Garth. Suddenly she is tormented by worry. What if the girlfriend is some seventeen-year-old bimbo stoned on coke who will have Garth snorting with them? There are some practical steps this mother can take to check out the situation—but worry will do nothing but rob her of her week till she gets Garth back.

A thousand times a day, thoughts like that mother's cross our minds. They don't settle anything or change the course of events, but they do waste our time. They do divert us from more positive thoughts. Worrying is one of the most common thinking errors. Fortunately, it responds well to the technique of *Stopping*. Order each worrisome thought to STOP, and gradually you'll break your Inner Voice of the habit. As the worries disappear, your life will become unbelievably more pleasant.

Vincent, a hard-working bachelor in his late twenties, was a middle-management executive in a large company. His mother had died when he was young, and his father had raised him. They had gotten along famously, more or less taking care of each other, the only drawback—a slight one—being that the father had tended to be overprotective, filling Vincent's head with many thoughts of all the things he should worry about.

Without realizing it, Vincent had carried these with him into his adult life. His Inner Voice had successfully taken over his father's role. Vincent was a worrier.

Although he was strongly attracted to a young woman in his department, he never got around to asking her for a date. His worries took over. "It's not a good idea to date someone you work with." "If she says no, it'll be embarrassing." "I saw her chatting with Dick at the water cooler this morning. Maybe she's dating him."

Don't let futile worries immobilize you. Train yourself to differentiate between legitimate concerns and futile self-torment. If your worry is something you can do something about, fine: Do it. For example, if you find yourself wondering whether you're handling a job correctly, analyze the situation, get advice if you can, and take some action. That's productive. If you're worried about a cosmic eventuality, STOP.

As for Vincent, he came for I.S.T. about another matter entirely, and in the course of it, he got an unexpected bonus. When he Listened In, he heard the useless pile-up of worries that were restricting him. He Underlined the weakening thoughts. And he Stopped his Inner Voice. When he had sufficiently dammed that stream of worries, he asked the young woman in his office out. Not only did she accept, she asked her own question: "Vincent, what took you so long?"

Now practice the *Stopping* technique with some of your thoughts: Which of the following give you difficulty with persistent thoughts that you want to *Stop*?

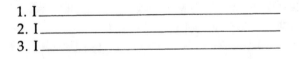

		Practice Stopping
Do you hear?	1. "I can't do it. . . ."	STOP
	2. "I'm lousy at. . . ."	STOP
	or	
You fill in	3. "I'm_____. . . ."	STOP
	4. "I_____. . . ."	STOP

Pick one of your undesirable thoughts and practice stopping it several times a day. Keep track of your successes and failures. Try *Listening In* to other types of thoughts—ones that depress or inhibit you. List the three recurring things you keep thinking *about* but believe you can't *stop*:

1. I_____

2. I_____

3. I_____

Now, after each time the thought occurs, train yourself to *overpower the thought* with a more intriguing and attractive one.

Why does *Stopping* work? The answer is incredibly simple. YOU CAN THINK OF ONLY ONE THING AT A TIME. If you can lock the word STOP in your thinking space (your Inner Speech Center), there is *no room* for the negative thought.

SUMMING UP

The biggest advantage I.S.T. gives you is that it's *always at hand*. You don't have to go to a gym or rehearsal hall to practice. Wherever *you* are, your thoughts are. You can Listen In and Underline all through the day. And now that you know how, you can put *Stopping* to work.

Although you learned these three techniques separately, the second advantage of the system is that they combine naturally and well. As you become more accustomed to *Stopping*, you'll be able to intervene more quickly and merge the three steps until they become practically simultaneous. In the meantime, continue to review each step individually and keep these points in mind about *Stopping*:

1. When a negative message starts, Stop it as *soon* as you can.
2. Use the one-word command, STOP.
3. Be forceful. Take charge. Don't allow the bad news to continue.
4. Say the word STOP out loud when you can. It strengthens your position.

5. Practice until you can Stop the thought earlier each time you try.
6. Be on the alert for the most persistent messages.
7. Brake—the—thought. Slow—it—down—so—you—hear—it—clearly.

Integrate what you have learned so far, and proceed to Technique #4: What do you do after you Stop?

CHAPTER 7

INNER SPEECH TECHNIQUE #4:
SWITCHING
CHANGING THE CONTENT
OF YOUR INNER SPEECH

Do not just Stop your damaging inner speech and leave yourself with an empty head! Move on immediately to master:

POWER THINKING TECHNIQUE #4: SWITCHING

Switching is deliberately to interrupt damaging inner speech and replace it with *positive* internal voices.

So far we've discussed the first three techniques of Inner Speech Therapy. You've learned to hear what's going on in your head (*Listening In*); to isolate the damaging messages (*Underlining*); and to stop them as soon as they begin (*Stopping*). But what happens after you exorcise the demons? Minds don't stay empty. They fill up of their own accord, and that's precisely what you don't want yours to do. And unless you replace the damaging thought, it will return. That is a key point to remember.

WHAT IS SWITCHING?

One person described *Switching* this way: "Every night, I lie in bed, frantic to fall asleep, but kept awake by a whirlpool of thoughts that keep spinning, spinning, spinning around in my head. It's as if my mind is out of control, and I'm being carried along with it. These are never constructive thoughts. They rehash yesterday. Could I have done something better? Was I too harsh with the children? I forgot to return the client's call.

"From yesterday I go to tomorrow and an equally senseless bombardment. I hear my thoughts fighting with each other over the way to handle matters that in all likelihood will never arise. I'm completely wrung out from all this activity. And then—finally, when I'm just about at my wits' end—something happens. I hear my own voice break in, saying, Stop! Cut it out! What are you doing to yourself? Haven't you had enough? Think about the wonderful day you had with Jenny at the zoo. Remember how she laughed at those chimps?

"Soon my head is filled with pleasant memories, my thoughts slow down, and I'm able to fall asleep. Sometimes it takes quite a few Stops and Switches, but it works if I keep working it."

That's *Switching*: replacing bad thoughts with good ones. It can happen spontaneously, as in the case just described, or it can be an intentional act on your part. Be sure to keep in mind that *Switching* can be intentional, that it can be learned. With a little diligence, you can train yourself to be good at it. Here are some tips on going about it.

First, remember that *Stopping* and *Switching* go

hand in hand. As soon as you hear an undesirable thought, break in with the *Stopping* technique. Cut off the thought as early as you can and as many times as you have to. Some thoughts are doggedly persistent, but you can be more so.

Think of yourself in the position of the telephone operator who breaks in to tell you, "Your time is up. Deposit another quarter, please." If you continue talking, she breaks in a second time. The third time, the line goes dead. You have to persevere with *Stopping* in the same way, not harshly, but firmly. If you do, the negative thought will fade. You'll be able to replace it with something more helpful.

The more quickly that *Switching* fills the void left by Stopping, the more effective it will be. Empty periods of mind time breed trouble. Try to be ready to fill any gaps with a *Switching* sentence you've prepared in advance. Think of something now and memorize it, so it will be available when you need it. Here are some examples of the kind of thing that works: "I'll switch to thinking about the promotion I got. I said, 'This means a lot to me,' and he said, 'You mean a lot to us.'" "I'll switch to thinking about that day in the mountains. Next time I'm going to take the other trail, clear to the top."

Be sure your *Switching* sentence is something that gives you pleasure or fortifies you in some way. The importance of what we think about has been understood since ancient times. In the words of the Bible, "Whatever is honorable... whatever is lovely... whatever is gracious... think about these things."

In one true story, the *Switching* was crucial. The patient, Joanna, was a capable woman with a history of recurrent, severe depressions which even included occasional thoughts of suicide. Her Inner Speech was filled with depressing thoughts:

"Nothing has ever gone right for me."
"I have nothing to show for my life."

Then it happened that she went to see James Stewart in the movie *It's a Wonderful Life*. Joanna was no James Stewart, and she hadn't done nearly as many wonderful things for her community as he had done in the movie. But from that time, she and her therapist began to Switch to thinking to what she *had* done, and *planned* to do in her life. When she made a list of the contributions she had made in life, it was not spectacular, no awards nor special honors. But there were the accomplishments of a basically good person who had performed the services that came her way, volunteering for some, pressed into service by necessity in others. Like many "good" people, she judged herself far too harshly, never feeling she measured up to her own standards.

The Stewart movie helped her decide that she could Switch her usual thoughts about herself. In therapy she had been exposed to the idea that whenever she was depressed, it was because she was allowing herself to have a pessimistic thought about herself, and her life. The movie gave her a scenario to follow. Her Switch was to James Stewart, and then to herself. It lifted her spirits because she could count events in her life that were not failures. She thought about those things.

She Switched her thoughts. Eventually, using therapy, she retrained her thinking so that she could Switch her depressing thoughts almost as soon as they began. She remembered happy occasions. When she wasn't burdened throughout her days and nights with thoughts of failure she had more energy to do things that were productive.

If your mind is obsessed with *negative thoughts,* you can interrupt your thinking and control its flow (*Listening In, Underlining, Stopping*). You will then move in a positive direction (*Switching*).

If your mind is filled with self-assured thoughts, you can control the thinking and *not allow negative Switching to happen.* The secret is in observing how you think; learning how your thoughts flow and change, and training yourself to Switch thoughts in mid-flow. You can improve your mental life and you can avoid Pitfalls.

A Pitfall occurs when you hear your own inner speech interrupted *by an undesirable voice that belongs to someone else.* That voice takes over your thinking.

You are anticipating a first-time visit from a congenial pen-pal from the Coast. Your plans are interrupted by a voice suggesting:

"How do you know he's not married?"

Or you hear your parents:

"What are the neighbors going to think?"

Are your neighbors thinking? Have you ever known what they think? When you really get down to it—what is more important? *Your* thinking, or your neighbors'? You will feel better if you Switch whenever you find yourself the victim of such pitfalls.

The pitfalls to watch for most carefully are the inner monologues that put you down and damage your self-respect. This kind of thinking usually features Over-personalizing, a troublemaker which accomplishes nothing. It only makes you feel insecure. And it is insecure people make the most errors in their thinking and in their relationships.

Over-personalizing is blaming *yourself* for everything that happens in a relationship; feeling that if anything goes wrong, it must be *your* fault. To recognize Over-personalizing, look for Voice Thoughts like these: "Why didn't he call? There must be something the matter with me—I don't wear well on people." Have you noticed which words to Underline? *Must. The matter with me.* Those words don't do you a bit of good. Stop them. Then Switch to a more purposeful thought. "I'll wash my hair, so I'll look good tomorrow. Or "I'll call Betsy. She's always full of news and bright ideas."

Another way we Over-personalize is with thoughts like this one: "She can't do this to me." Can't she? Well, don't bet on it. She just did. The harmful part of that thought is the "to me." Did she do whatever she did because you're you? Probably not. More likely, she did it because that's the kind of thing she does, and you happened to be there. If you were to investigate, you'd be apt to find she "does it" to everyone. So stop Over-personalizing. That kind of thinking often leads to a vicious cycle that needs to be interrupted.

Brooding is another danger area, composed of thoughts that cause pain and go on too long. "How could he have treated me that way after all we went through together?" "Why did I get passed over for a raise with all the overtime I put in?" These are unanswerable, debilitating thoughts that sap your strength. Break in on them. Stop them. Talk back to them. Intervene with your own *Switching* question.

Ask your Inner Voice, "What are you doing to me? I have better thoughts to think." Then go ahead and think them.

Speculation is another way we torture ourselves. "What will I do if the company's lease expires and they move out of town?" Switch immediately to, "It's silly to worry about that now. There's a good program on." Not that it has to be TV, of course. That's only an example of something that will occupy your mind in a less punishing way. The secret is not to remain passive, but to take some sort of active stance. Give your mind new scenarios to follow so the old thoughts can't crowd back in.

Switching Effectively

Distracting yourself is helpful while you're practicing the *Switching* technique. But *Switching* is most effective when you can be instructive in your replacement thoughts. For instance, if you hear, "I'll never be able to do that," it isn't enough just to intervene with, "Stop. I can do that." That's too vague, too easy a generalization. Merely saying you can cope won't necessarily cause it to happen. You'll make much more progress if you break your statements down into specific suggestions. "I'm patient. I can figure this out. I'll see if there's a book in the library that will help me." Or, "I've done harder things in my life. Maybe I'll have to work it out by trial and error, but I'll give it my best shot." Thoughts like those take longer, but they constitute healthy thinking. They allow you to break a problem down into workable parts.

Perhaps you're having money problems. Your Inner

Voice takes you to task. You hear it saying, "I spend money as fast as I earn it." Look behind that. Do you hear something else? Is an echo of a parent's critical voice coming through asking, "Do you have to spend it just because you've got it?" Tell that critical voice to Stop. Switch your own voice to, "I want to figure out how to budget."

That's positive *Switching*, the kind that leads to solutions. Once you've gotten that far, you can break your problem down into more manageable parts. "I've had trouble dealing with money in the past. I don't put enough aside for future needs." Get even more specific. "If I calculate how much my vacation is going to cost, and save a percentage of it each week, I'll enjoy it more when the time comes."

BENEVOLENT VOICES

We want to stress the importance of sorting out the voices in your head. Often, the spontaneous *Switching* you do is in the useful voice of a Benevolent Friend. This can be any one of a number of people: a current buddy, a friend from the past, a mentor at work, a teacher, a kindly uncle or aunt, a grandparent, an understanding sibling, a therapist. It can be one of your parents. Whoever it is, it's a voice you want to keep. It's usually helpful, interested, often more experienced than you are, and a patient guide through a difficult time.

The Benevolent Friend treats you as you would treat a person of whom you were very fond. It's someone who helps you interrupt the negative flow in your mind by substituting a more positive voice. Eventually you yourself should be your Benevolent Friend, ready to intercede in your own behalf. The goal of I.S.T. is to train your own Inner Voice for this role. Let's say, for instance, you hear that old negative voice at work: "Why does everyone take advantage of me?" Stop. Now substitute a benevolent voice with a *Switching* thought: "Not everyone takes advantage. You have good friends who do come through for you. Think this one through again."

A change in your thinking automatically changes your feelings. Your life is controlled by your thinking, which is why *Switching* is so significant. When you are at your best, and feeling good, you know you can think anything you want to think. Once you've mastered the *Switching* technique, you have a tool that is always at your disposal that helps you take charge of your thinking directly.

TAKEOVERS

These days, we're all familiar with Takeovers, especially if we read the business pages of our daily newspaper. Dozens of companies have been appropriated by other firms, some in friendly transactions, others in moves that are termed "hostile." Our minds are subject to hostile Takeovers, too, and we can spare ourselves much suffering by being on the alert for them.

Takeovers are instances of negative *Switching*, times when your own Inner Speech is interrupted by an undesirable voice that belongs to somebody else, an alien voice that takes over your thinking. You might be feeling great, contemplating an exciting sexual experience when all of a sudden that critical voice erupts with, "What if my timing is off?" The rapture fades, and you're left with the dark cloud of a thought that you'll fail your partner.

If your mind is filled with self-assured thoughts, you'll be able to prevent Takeovers. The secret is in observing how you think, learning how your thoughts flow and change, and training yourself to Switch to helpful thoughts in mid-flow. Rid yourself of Takeovers.

Here is an exercise for you. You think the thought:

"I've never been so happy with anybody."

Then your next thought suddenly appears:

"What if the relationship doesn't last?"

Now, using Inner Speech Training, how would you help yourself at that moment?

SUMMING UP

Of the four steps we've discussed so far, *Switching* is by far the most powerful. It bolsters you by reducing the painful pressures your Inner Voice has been putting on you. *Switching* can be learned, but it requires vigilance. You'll want to keep the following pointers in mind as you practice it.

1. Make a habit of *Listening In* and *Underlining*. They keep you aware.
2. As soon as you hear an unwanted thought, Stop it. If the thought persists, Stop it as many times

as you need to, always trying to intervene as early as possible.

3. Talk to yourself in a sympathetic voice. You can Stop unwanted dialogues more easily if you're not judgmental.

4. Have a *Switching* thought ready to substitute for the thought you've just stopped.

5. Break your thoughts down into achievable parts. Be as specific as you can.

6. Be on the lookout for unfriendly, critical voices. They have no right to invade your thoughts. Don't be one of those people who automatically Switches your thinking to something grim when you are feeling good.

7. Make the most of any help you get from a benevolent friend.

8. Don't be discouraged if you have a failure or two. You're learning a new way of thinking and that takes time.

CHAPTER 8

INNER SPEECH TECHNIQUE #5:
REORIENTING
DIRECTING YOUR THINKING
TO A DIFFERENT GOAL

Have you ever been tired and down late in the day, and someone said, "Let's go out"?

Your spirits picked up, and you began thinking about washing your face, putting on some fresh clothes, and hearing music in your head.

That is the experience of *Reorienting*. You reoriented the direction of your thinking. Your mood changed as you began to focus on a different target. The thing that produced your new enthusiasm was a reoriented *thought*. This is the power of Technique #5: *Reorienting*.

POWER THINKING TECHNIQUE #5: REORIENTING

Reorienting is to change the direction of your thinking. Your thinking deliberately focuses on a different target. If you are preparing for a takeoff when flying, you can Reorient your thinking from whether the engines will fail to what you are going to do when you are in Boston.

Change the direction of your thinking and you will change the direction you move today—and every day from now on. When you are in trouble, find a *directing circumstance that positively demands your attention.*

Sylvia R. had a severe fear of going outside and being alone (agoraphobia). Despite therapy, she had barely improved. She needed some practical techniques to combine with the insights she had already learned.

We suggested that Sylvia Reorient her thoughts when she went out marketing. She agreed that each time she went, she would make a complete list of what she had to do. Then when she finally got outside (although she still felt anxious), she refocused and Reoriented her attention to a recording of precisely what she had to do. Using all the willpower she could muster, she kept her thoughts on what she was doing that very moment: ("Salad dressing, in Aisle 5; now Produce, for broccoli—on sale—and a cantaloupe, if ripe"). By retraining her thought patterns, she eventually was able to go outside by herself with enough thinking power to overcome her anxiety.

Reorient yourself right now. You are tense because you have a deadline and must finish a huge project by Friday. Now Reorient: On Saturday you plan to have fun by going shopping with your friends. Your project will be completed and you will have the day off.

Reorient from "Friday workload" to "Saturday fun." Your feelings will follow your new Reoriented thoughts if you practice seeking out different, more attractive goals. It takes training to Reorient from preoccupation with an ordeal to prospects that are pleasurable.

Also practice this technique to Reorient away from painful anxiety to *an active, problem-solving framework.*

For example, the next time your plane is landing, get yourself interested in the pattern of lights and roads near the airport, and the structures on the ground. Think about some activity on the ground that absorbs you and pulls your thinking to that subject.

If you concentrate on your *fear*—of elevators, crowds, or being rejected by a friend—you could panic.

If you choose to concentrate on some *attractive goal* and actively *change the focus* of your attention, you will feel much more in command, calmer, and more competent.

Visualize yourself doing a job well. Once people learned that they could do better by watching successful rehearsals in their minds, they were able to hit a golf ball better, improve their skiing, and almost immediately cope with all sorts of physical activity that had previously frustrated them. They Reoriented from a clumsy, inept image of themselves to a smooth, professional one.

Reorienting means to *see yourself managing successfully* in a stressful situation. It is a *rehearsal in your mind* in which you vividly picture yourself handling a difficult issue with methods well chosen to see you through. For example, you see yourself riding to the eighth floor in an elevator, and practicing healthy thinking techniques when the elevator doors close. You can visualize yourself making love with your partner. You hold and stroke each other and find each other's mouths, kissing deeply.

Reorient yourself by visualizing that you are handling with aplomb some of the encounters in your life that make you anxious or depressed. Important: Don't be simplistic—visualize the detailed techniques by which you meet every phase of the occasion.

Reorienting worked very well for Suzanne B. She was a severely depressed executive secretary who was suffering from what is termed a depressing triad—she gathered evidence from the past, present, and future that nothing had gone right, was going right, or would ever go right. By using her patterns of repetitive cognitions, she locked herself into a severely depressed state and intensified it by her misperception of what was going on around her.

She viewed everything in a negative light. The most trivial event was always interpreted by her depressive style to portend something ominous.

In therapy, Suzanne B. was asked to make a list of what made her feel *good*—not an easy task for her. It had to be emphasized that she could include anything, no matter how insignificant. The list was initially a short one. It included hiking, watching certain television shows, and hand-painting her own greeting cards. She was asked to spend more time doing these small things that gave her pleasure and to record how she felt afterwards. When she started to note relaxed or cheerful feelings, she was able to keep focusing on the things that she enjoyed and to stop using her former approach of examining every event pessimistically. Thus, in small but positive steps, her depression dwindled away.

Reorienting helped Suzanne B. see herself as less helpless than before, and with visual rehearsal she soon had more confidence to go out and mix successfully with her fellow hikers. Her "helpless" self-concept changed to the point where she realized that she was not helpless, and with that change in outlook, she became less depressed.

Switching and *Reorienting* have much in common. But there is an important difference. You will find it useful when you are either anxious or depressed to follow all the way to this fifth I.S.T. step of *Reorienting*.

Switching is an immediate thinking technique which should follow immediately after *Stopping*. *Stopping* alone is not enough, because your mind abhors a vacuum, and some thought will arrive momentarily and fill that vacuum if you do not deliberately choose what thought you want to occupy your mind. Your conscious choice of a useful thought will be far more helpful than letting an old automatic thought take over. Chapter 7 described how the best *Switching* is toward an idea that begins to solve the immediate problem at hand. If that is not possible at the moment, then it is valuable for you to have some pleasant and successful thoughts memorized in advance to Switch into place. Eventually, those affirming thoughts about yourself and your world can become your automatic thoughts. Many people, of course, do not believe that comforting thoughts can ever become automatic. You were not born with your thought patterns. You learned them. And if some of those habitual thoughts are not doing you much good, you can learn a different and more serviceable pattern of inner speech.

Bill is a man who is no wiser nor dumber than the average person. He makes his share of mistakes. He once remarked to his therapist that he probably does 10,000 different things in a week. Those include things like tying his shoes, taking a milk carton out of the refrigerator, driving to work, writing a letter, trying to settle an argument between his two children, making love, balancing his checkbook, trying to make some sense out of the conflicts in Northern Ireland, and so on. So he is like most people.

Bill has never tried to figure out how many mis-

takes he makes in a week, but he knows that the number adds up. He has learned to do something constructive for himself when he makes a mistake. He pays attention to the mistake, gives it some thought, and then thinks something like this: "That isn't like you, Bill. You don't want to do that. Next time I will_____."
And then Bill thinks of a better way to do the thing at which he just made a mistake. He coaches himself gently. His I.S.T. has paid off for him. He accepts that mistakes are a part of life. *Switching* has helped him acknowledge his mistakes in a way that corrects them and keeps him from belittling himself.

Reorienting, in contrast to *Switching*, is a much broader technique. You can Reorient to a grander view of your life. You can learn to see yourself differently. You can learn to see the world around you differently, in big and little ways.

Pete was a lineman for a college football team that was playing for the national championship on a November Saturday afternoon. The game was close, the stakes were especially enormous for Bill, because he was the team captain. He broke his leg during a play in the third quarter of the game. He continued to play the rest of the game and never felt any pain until the game was over.

How could this be? The answer is that Bill was so oriented toward winning the game, and playing his part in it, that he literally paid no conscious attention to his broken leg and felt no pain. When he returned to the locker room after the game, the pain became so great that he writhed on the floor crying. Did the pain not exist until the game was over? You may answer that for yourself in any way that makes sense to you. The fact is that Bill felt no pain. His focus on the game completely blocked it.

That is a true story, and it has been duplicated countless times in the lives of people who were oriented toward goals that totally dominated their thinking so that no other thought or sensation could make its way into their consciousness.

In an episode parallel to that of Bill's, a ballerina finished dancing *Coppelia* with a broken ankle. Granted, there are physiologic factors that also could be adduced for delayed reaction to trauma. But our point here is that if you set your thoughts on a goal that is worthy of your best self, you will be so drawn to do your best that you will block out some of the crippling thoughts that have held you back.

Reorienting is akin to Imaging. We prefer the term *Reorienting* because it implies a larger vision of yourself, and a wider view of your possibilities. It is important to Image your goals. It is even more helpful to Reorient and see yourself as a person who can control more and more of your life by controlling your thinking.

You can Reorient around an optimistic frame of reference. If you think you can do anything, you increase your chances of doing it. A Reorientation toward optimism gets you moving. In contrast, depressing thoughts bog you down and stymie you, because you are thinking "What's the use?"

Optimists keep trying, because they believe they can reach their goal. This is not mindless daydreaming. An optimist tries. A daydreamer just daydreams.

You can make it a habit of remembering your best self, your best inner speech, your best images of the you that you want to be. Reorient yourself toward the best (and honest) compliments that you have received in your life. Remember particularly those things about which you have consistently been complimented.

That's the real you. Make that the frame of reference for your life. Now you are creating a new orientation, a new image of yourself. This is who you want to be. If you think it, you can make more and more of it come true for yourself. You know you have often made yourself feel miserable because of what you thought. It works the same the other way. A picture of your best self, of you at your best, of you the way you have always wanted to be—will pull you along in that direction.

Reorienting works like a magnet. Picture yourself reaching your goals, and you will feel the tug of the magnet pulling you.

Here are three ways to Reorient your thinking—and your life—thoughts that build you up, not put you down:

1. Think of a truly helpful compliment that you once received. You then Reorient toward *your assets*.
2. Think of what is genuinely important to you. You then Reorient toward *satisfying feelings*.
3. Think of something to be excited about. You then Reorient toward *stimulating goal-directed ideas*.

Write down the three right now. Then you will have them ready the next time that you need to Reorient.

Think of_____

Think of_____

Think of_____

Now you have the five basics of Power Thinking, ready to put to use.

INTERMISSION

TEN POWERFUL THINGS YOU CAN DO RIGHT NOW

You've learned the five crucial steps of the Inner Speech system. What are you going to do with them?

The most natural tendency is already in your mind. A small but overbearing voice. "Okay. Now I can take a break."

On the contrary, it's now time to start, if you want to change your life, so change that thought. Let the corrective power of Inner Speech Training go to work for you by immediately instituting a simple series of steps in your everyday life.

The first thing to do is to start keeping a continuous updated record of your erroneous thinking.

Most people usually get the best results with the use of a small diary to record their weakening repetitive thoughts. Buy a small 3×5 notebook that you can carry with you. Then circle the most damaging negative parts of these thoughts. Use your new knowledge to ascertain exactly which part is most damaging.

Example: The thought, "Is that all there is in my

life?" Try changing it to "What else can I put in my life?"

Here now are the ten powerful things you can do—right now.

1. STOP ALL-OR-NOTHING THINKING

Quiz yourself. Do you tend to think in extremes or absolutes? "I have to be first." "I'm nothing but a slob." "I have to have the most." "Nothing works for me." Those thoughts will make you suffer. Underline those extremes and Stop.

2. AVOID OVERGENERALIZING

This can best be done by underlining all the universalizing (the everythings and forevers) you hear in your mind. Then work on *Stopping* them. The cliché "Never say never" is good advice.

3. LISTEN IN ACCURATELY TO THE FEEDBACK FROM YOUR BODY

Signals from your body need to be listened to, and then accurately interpreted. Let your body feed your mind, but with good stuff. When your body is tired, it is telling you something. What are the thoughts that accompany the tiredness? Listen. The thought may be saying "Do something nice for yourself." Other times, your body will be giving you a pleasure message. Go with it. Think of the pleasure your body has given you throughout your life. Yes, sometimes your body has ached, too, but you will do something wonderful for your mood if you think about the wonderful feelings your body has brought you.

4. THINK IN MICROSTEPS

Solve a problem by breaking it down into the smallest possible steps—steps so small that anyone could take them, like putting one foot in front of the other. Then as you work on the little picture with microsteps, you can eventually Switch to the big picture, put together with many microsteps. One hundred quantitative steps (that is, one hundred changes in your thoughts) will bring a qualitative change in your feeling about yourself and about your life.

5. MINIMIZE YOUR MAGNIFICATIONS

Do not exaggerate your thinking. "It was the worst thing I ever heard." "I was totally crushed." "I nearly died." "I was destroyed." "I thought I'd explode." No such things happened. Those are thoughts that produce helpless feelings about yourself. You deserve to think better of yourself.

6. MONITOR THE WAR BETWEEN YOUR THOUGHTS

Some quarreling between your thoughts is an important part of thinking. It develops judgment. But if your mind is a constant battlefield, Listen In and identify the different voices and thoughts so you can decide whose to Stop. If your thoughts go round and round, you are only repeating yourself, and not moving on to finding the solution to the problem. When you're caught up in circular thinking, that is a signal to Stop and come at things from a different angle.

7. KEEP YOUR THOUGHTS IN YOUR OWN VOICE

When you have conflicts, Underline your own internal voice. Then Stop the unwanted voice of someone else. We have spoken of the reservoir of common sense deep inside you. Abide by its voice. We do not mean that every impulse you have should be acted on. We are referring to your "measured judgment." You have relied on it countless times. You know the tone of voice of your inner common sense. Those are the thoughts to act on.

8. AVOID OVERLOOKING

Do you perceive all that you are capable of perceiving? Choose not to think the stressful thoughts because they block you from seeing things from a deep and wide perspective. Take a laugh break. Change a losing pattern. Get outside yourself. Imagine that you are Bertrand Russell. How would he perceive your situation?

9. THINK "MAINTENANCE OR MISSION?"

Some people usually think "maintenance" thoughts; that is like straightening up your sock

drawer. Others usually think "mission thoughts"; those
are thoughts that move you ahead, such as planning a
project that will bring you a satisfying new experience.
Maintenance is about cleaning up the past. Mission is
moving ahead. When you find yourself thinking about
a maintenance task, nudge yourself over into a mission
task.

10. KEEP YOUR THINKING GOAL DIRECTED

Most systems work less well than our expectations.
Don't waste your time with the critical voices holding
you back. Monitor your inner speech to keep your goals
clear. Direct yourself in your own strong voice: "This is
where I want to go."

CHAPTER 9

POWER SHIFTING
STRENGTHENING YOUR INNER SPEECH

And Lucy said:

> "You, Charlie Brown, are a foul ball in the line
> drive of life. You're in the shadow of your own
> goal posts...You are a miscue...You are
> three putts on the eighteenth green...You are
> a seven-ten split in the tenth frame...A love
> set. You have dropped a rod and reel in the
> lake of life...You are a missed free throw, a
> shanked nine iron, and a called third strike."

Have you mastered enough Power Thinking techniques to see what the trouble is, and how to change it,
for poor Charlie Brown? If Charlie's thinking about
himself contains Lucy's words, he is in big trouble!

If you are getting some help already from the five
basic techniques, you are ready to go on to your own
more powerful thinking. Here are ways to strengthen
your mind by alerting yourself to the content and character of your inner speech—and then shifting to Power.

1. Is Your Internal Speech Merely a Repeat of Your Childhood Thinking?

You wouldn't want Lucy's voice talking in your head. Too many times, your mind may be filled with other people's voices talking to you as if you were a six-year-old, saying nasty things about you.

Can you remember hearing, earlier in your life, the voice of a mother who apparently believed you didn't have the sense to come in out of the rain:

> "Could you please try and take care of yourself? You know how you tend to catch cold."

Or,

> "You never had any sense of time. I understand that that's the way you are, but it makes such a bad impression because it looks so rude and inconsiderate."

You may need to shift the character of your inner speech and start listening to your *own* voice.

We should be doing the speaking for ourselves— especially *internally*, where it counts the most.

Practice listing the voices that you hear in your head. When you are thinking, does your inner speech sound like a recording of someone else's words? Here is an exercise to help you Listen In, so you can hear whether your inner voices are your voice, or someone else's, and whether the voices are helpful or harmful.

Review your memories of each of the persons listed. The way to do this is to remember the words and the tone of voice of these people. Pay close attention also to the feeling you get when you think of one of these people saying something to you. Let's begin with two easy examples:

What does the voice of a best friend sound like in your mind?

What does the voice of a worst enemy sound like in your mind?

Now you are ready to go on to the others. What is the image of each of these people in your mind? Do the words of each of these people do something for you or against you?

	Positive influence	Negative influence
Mother		
Father		
Husband/wife		
Boy/girlfriend		
Child		
Teacher		
Boss		
Clergy		
Best friend		
Worst enemy		
Childhood rival		
Coach		
Special lingering voice		

The key to being your own person is to monitor your own inner voice. Be sure that the words and thoughts are your *own* thoughts. You will when you are at your best. The more familiar you are with your mature inner voice, the quicker you will be able to recognize unwanted voices when they are disguised as your own.

Find the missing voice in the following case:

Cathy B. came into therapy because of a "depression." She had just broken up for the third time with her boyfriend. He said he couldn't marry her because she was still too dependent on her mother and helping with her invalid father. Her mind was a ménage à trois. Endless conversations occurred between Frank, her boyfriend, her mother, and occasionally even her own small voice—dialogues that reflected the conflicts between the two polarizing forces in her life.

Boyfriend's voice	Mother's voice
"I've got to go to Palm Springs for this conference. Why don't you come along? I won't be working the whole time, and it would be a change for you—you could use a dose of sun."	"He's so manipulative. He's always putting pressure on you..."
"I'm getting heavy into Chinese cooking. Why don't you come over tonight and check out my moo goo gai pan."	"He's not very honest about saying what he's really got in mind..."

Cathy's voice
"I can't decide..."

Cathy B. felt so depressed that she couldn't concentrate on her job. She had taken a mild tranquilizer
to help her with her anxieties, but she still felt terribly
upset most of the time.

The real problem in this case was the *Missing
Voice*—and it was Cathy's *own voice*. Two contrasting
voices were making opposing demands on her, and she
was in constant conflict as to which one to obey. Her
boyfriend's and her mother's voices were in her head
almost constantly, trying to control her mind. This led
to a neurotic conflict between two different voices, and
Cathy B. was unable to make up her mind.

In therapy, Cathy B. was able to listen in to their
voices, work on *Stopping* them, and then switch to listening to her own healthy thinking.

Every time she heard her mother's voice inside her
head, she would recognize it and say "Stop." Then she
carefully thought her own thoughts about Frank. She
would ask herself, "What do *I* really think? What is best
for *me*? What do *I* want? What is in *my* best interests?
Knowing Frank as I do, what are my honest thoughts
about him?"

The answers to these questions helped her to do
her own thinking. Sometimes her thoughts were the
same as her mother's thoughts. Sometimes her
thoughts were the same as Frank's. She didn't have to
reject their thoughts just for the sake of being contrary.
But when she did find her own thoughts, she knew they
were her thoughts, and she didn't feel manipulated by
anyone else. It was the emergence, finally, of an independent voice.

Do your parents dominate your inner speech? Start
with your childhood. Can you remember a voice that
said, "Don't stand under a tree in a thunderstorm."

"Don't go anywhere with anyone, even if they say I've been in an accident and they're supposed to get you." Without such a voice, you probably couldn't have survived in a complex world.

In adolescence, the voices started to change. There were more dialogues and often angry exchanges. The adolescent fought back the attempts of parents to guide via mind control.

Can you recall discussions in your head like: "What do you know about what's okay for kids? It's Saturday night and all the other kids are staying out late—" And the inevitable inner voice when the hands of the clock got near midnight—"It's time to go home—I'm late—I've got to find a phone." Or even more controlling were the early forays of sexuality—"Are you sure you feel you're ready to handle this?" Your mother's voice, cautioning you through your sexual experience, and often lingering when you perhaps didn't want her presence in your mind. "I don't care how much things change, people always judge the *girl!*"

Finally, as we mature, the voices become more complex and intricate. Witness the surgical resident about to perform a difficult operation. In her head she can hear the voice of her mentors guiding her through each tedious, necessary step:

> "Make sure you tie off *all* the bleeders before going into the peritoneum."

These voices are necessary for our continued education and growth. We get them from our teachers, our parents, the people around us, and even worthy books. The sounder the teaching, the better the voices guide us through the complexities of human, sexual, and professional life.

2. DO GUILT-RIDDEN VOICES DOMINATE YOUR INNER SPEECH?

You may be controlled by the neurotic thinking of others in more immediate ways. Consider going to the movies with an obsessive personality, and you are required to share his worry about whether or not he parked the car in a legal space and won't be towed away. "I'm not sure, but I *think* I parked the car in a no-parking zone. I'll probably get a ticket. For what that'll cost, we could have done a Broadway play."

"Step on a crack, break your grandmother's back." "Tattle-Tale Tit/Your tongue shall be slit/And all the dogs in our town/Shall have a little bit." One reason such rhymes stick in our minds is that they dramatize childhood guilt. Guilt is on children's minds most of the time, although they do a pretty good job of concealing that fact from their parents. Most children at the age of nine would like to change their first names, because they heard their first names used most often in a way that put guilt, shame, or fear into their minds. "Jimmy, you get in here right now." "Billy, you're filthy." "Melissa, look at you!" "Matthew, you're a disgrace." "Ellen, you should be ashamed."

Guilt is built in during the ordinary traditional experiences of childhood. This is why the critical voices haunt one's conscious thought. Those guilt-producing voices are most apt to sound like your parents' voices. But many of you will say, "My parents weren't really grim. I had a pretty good childhood. And I was always a pretty good girl." And when asked, "Did your parents expect you to be a good girl?"

"Oh boy, did they ever! But I didn't think I lived up to their expectations."

"How do you know that?"

"The voice in my head never lets me rest."

That is the inner voice that now needs to be examined in the light of your adult mind.

Many groups think they have a corner on guilt. There is Catholic guilt. There is Jewish guilt. There is the Protestant work ethic guilt. The fact is that no one escapes it, and many conventional patterns of thinking foster it. "Poor Mom! She never got to buy a new stick of furniture in her life, and she loved to try to make the place look cute." "Poor Pop. He never got to work in a field he loved." Actually, if Mom did wonders with Early Salvation Army, that was a triumph. Ernest Becker, in his last interview, said that a man who just supports his family is a hero. But, even if Mom and Pop did have it rough, we do not amend their deprivations by guilt-tripping ourselves. Their gallantry we can admire. Their self-pity we can sympathize with. Our admiration and our sympathy are worthier of them and of us than greeting-card guilt. The present-day task is to recognize guilt-tripping, and stop it when it is a useless mental tic.

The useful way to handle guilt is to *learn* from it. If you yourself were in error, if you were wrong, if you did make a mistake, then note it, think about how you can change it the next time you are faced with a similar situation. Then do not *harbor* it in your mind. Move on!

Your reservoir of common sense, to which we have referred, you know is there, because it has often led you to make effective decisions, and overrule destructive guilt. Hear your *own* voice. You can let the *best* part of you win the battle of the inner voices.

3. DOES YOUR THINKING SET YOU UP?

Do you hear yourself thinking, "I don't know what to do about invitations to Marcia and Phoebe, since they don't speak—" If you do this type of thinking, you set up defeating circumstances. A more productive stance is... *"While I still don't know what to do about inviting them, I am considering the possibilities. I will work it out by the time I have to mail the invitations."*

Self-fulfilling prophecies are as real as two plus two equals four. You can live out a failure prophecy, or a success prophecy. If you imagine that you will do well, superstition to the contrary, it will increase your chances of doing well. If you will increase the sense of *hope* in your thinking about a forthcoming performance, this will improve your behavior just as tangibly as taking a class in how to do the performance. Of course, it is important to do both: be hopeful for a happy outcome, and prepare wisely for it. But part of *wisdom* is to *hope* and *expect* to do well. Your behavior will imitate what you think about.

If you are trying to stop smoking, you can think about the next time someone offers you a cigarette. You can think to yourself: "That will be a rough moment. I probably will not be able to say no." That will set you up to increase your chances of failure. You also have the choice of preparing a better response in advance for the time someone offers you a cigarette: "No thank you. I am a nonsmoker." That script, when readied in your mind in advance of the test situation, will dramatically increase your chances of being the nonsmoker you want to be.

Your inner speech can be successfully combined with imaging yourself succeeding at whatever you plan to do. Our Olympic athletes use mental rehearsal to increase their agility. Tennis players have proven over and over again that it is not helpful for them to say to themselves before they serve, "I won't make an error," because that puts the word "error" in their minds. They will be more apt to succeed if they think before they serve, "The ball will go in."

4. DOES YOUR INNER SPEECH STAY IN THE PRESENT?

Examine your Inner Speech from the following time perspectives:
Inner statements about the past...

"Nothing ever went right for me."

Inner statements about the future...

"I'll never meet the right person."
"I'll never get the right job."

"How am I ever going to live when I retire if inflation keeps going on?" This was the thinking of a 27-year-old law school senior. He hadn't even *started* to earn a living and had already started to *worry* about the *distant* future.

Living in the present is a key to fulfillment and happiness. Your thinking exerts its greatest power when it deals in the present. For instance, let's look at "worry."

Worry is to think about what *might* possibly *happen*

in the *future*. Worry is a useless expenditure of your thought and time, because you cannot do anything useful by wondering, for example, if your husband will have a car accident while you are sitting at home.

Worry is not the same as constructive planning, which leads to constructive action. Worry focuses mental energy on situations that your mind cannot resolve; thus it is useless.

You are in control of this very moment. You cannot do anything to change yesterday. Tomorrow is not here, so you cannot live it now. But you have complete control over what you want to think at this very moment. You also have exciting freedom to do something right now. You can have the freedom to do many things that are satisfying, interesting, productive, relaxing, fun. You also have the freedom to do something or think something to make yourself miserable right now.

Take tiny steps in changing your thoughts right now and you will find that you will change how you feel. Take tiny steps that you know will succeed and you will accomplish something. Passive procrastination has no payoff that is worth having.

5. IS YOUR INNER SPEECH APPROPRIATE TO THE SITUATION?

Do you chronically overreact? Is your head filled with thoughts like:

"I'd like to kill him."

or

"If I can't have a new outfit, I rather skip the reception."

"Either they give me the raise or I walk off the job."

Are you hurting yourself by thinking inappropriate *angry* thoughts when the situation calls for *assertive* ones?

Check your Inner Speech to see if you *personalize* situations. A police car cruises up the block and you hear in your mind:

"Are they coming to notify me of an accident?"

Your husband is staring at a blond on television and you hear in your mind:

"Why aren't I always glamorous and irresistible?"

Your children are overtired and teasing each other, and you hear in your mind:

"Why aren't I the kind of mother who always makes the home peaceful and happy?"

The elevator man doesn't smile and you hear in your mind:

"Wasn't my Christmas tip enough?"

In each of these situations, there are probably several reasons why things are going wrong. Yet your mind has learned to behave inappropriately by taking every issue *personally*. Something *you* have done is not usually the cause of the problem in other people.

That kind of pessimism about oneself is a major factor in causing emotional depression. Current research in psychotherapy has proven that chronic pessimistic thinking can be changed with study and practice. Just as pessimism is a learned style of thinking, optimistic thinking can be learned. Take for example a worried thought like, "I guess I have no future." When *Listening In* to that thought, most people will immediately recognize that it is not useful nor helpful. The pessimism will persist, however, until the worrier catches on that he is hurting himself with that thought. Then he can substitute something of some value to him, which may either be a quick Switch to his vacation planning, or to a long-range Reorienting in which he sets some life goals that will create a future for him.

Inappropriate Inner Speech weakens your thinking and your ability to direct your life. To achieve control of your own mind and life, keep your internal voices in key with the actual situation; think in appropriate terms. Keep a perspective on each situation. Listen In: If you will take a moment to think *about* what you are thinking, you almost certainly will be able to tell yourself when you are overreacting.

Here is a reminder to encourage you to do your own Power Shifting: Every conscious act has an inner dialogue that accompanies it. You are thinking all of the time. You can Power Shift your life if you will concentrate on what you think and how you think.

Again, there is solid research evidence that to think constructively and to visualize a productive outcome will greatly enhance your success in whatever you do.

Remember the Five Power Shifts that have been developed in this chapter to train your Inner Speech to make your thinking more powerful:

1. Your internal speech should be in *your own adult voice*.
2. Your internal speech should not echo *childhood guilt*.
3. Your internal speech should not *set you up*.
4. Your internal speech should be *in the present*.
5. Your internal speech should be *appropriate to the given situation*.

CHAPTER 10

WHAT TYPE OF THINKER (PERSON) ARE YOU?
IDENTIFYING THE PERSONALITY PATTERNS IN YOUR INNER SPEECH

Where are you in your life? All of us reach our own turning points over and over in our lives; in fact, turning points may occur every time we choose what to think.

Critical choices occur daily, but you may simply fail to notice them. Therefore, you need to maintain an alert sense of your own thinking—to step aside and observe your Inner Speech, especially during these daily turning points.

This is the basis of I.S.T.: Your style of thinking (indeed, the very thoughts you think) influences your feelings and behavior which form the turning points in your life. The second point is that you *can* change your style of thinking.

This chapter offers you a checklist to discover persistent patterns in your thinking and to guide you in how to change your thinking—and yourself.

You have the choice to think what you want.

Each person develops a special "style" of thinking. This "style" is what we call *personality*. Generally, personality is identified by what is seen on the surface—

the characteristic patterns of feelings and behavior that differentiate one individual from another. However, the *reverse* is actually true: these characteristic personality traits develop from one's style of thinking when a particular voice dominates the inner speech.

This chapter and those that follow offer an opportunity to examine your patterns of thinking. We will describe six unproductive, perhaps even neurotic, styles of thinking: Anxious/Phobic, Obsessive, Depressive, Narcissistic, Masochistic, and Defensive/Detached. By the final chapter, you will also have learned about a seventh thinking style—a healthy one. You can learn how, with practice, to convert your negative patterns into effective ones that bring happiness to yourself and to those around you. You will see changes in your personality and outlook, and will be able to develop new ways to solve many of your problems. Keep in mind that one of the key words is "Switch." To Switch your thoughts is not as easy as to switch a light from off to on; but it is worth the effort to learn to do it with your thinking. *Switching* puts circumstances in a brighter, truer light. It is enlightening. People are constantly doing it by *Switching* thoughts.

The following checklist is designed to help you diagnose your thinking and personality patterns. There is no grade scale, not even a pass/fail. Its purpose is to enable you to get to know your thinking and yourself a bit better.

THE CHECKLIST

1. a. Is your panic button almost always on "Alert"?

   b. Does your mind scream "disaster" as you
      buckle the plane's seat belt?
   c. Do you tend to think your headaches are a
      sign of a brain tumor?
   d. Do you have trouble breathing in crowded
      or enclosed spaces?
   e. Do people say you overreact to things?
   f. Do frightening voices in your head freak
      you out?

2. a. Is your life largely blah?
   b. Do many things seem impossibly hard to
      do?
   c. Does your mind seem empty?
   d. Do you often wonder if you have a future?
   e. Is sex more trouble than it is worth?
   f. "The worst is yet to come." Could that be
      your motto?

3. a. Are you a prisoner of your thoughts?
   b. Is it tough for you to take a stand?
   c. Do repetitious concerns plague you?
   d. Are you too controlled?
   e. Are you quite stingy about showing your
      own feelings?
   f. Does a lingering anger occupy your
      thoughts?

4. a. Is it safer to be alone?
   b. Do you tend to regard an inquiry as an
      attack?
   c. Does your mind work overtime to one-up
      people?
   d. Do you feel it necessary to defend every de-
      cision you make?

e. Do you think self-sufficiency is of major importance?

f. Do you treasure being special and unique?

5. a. Do you feel sorry for yourself?

b. Is it hard for you to see yourself first in line?

c. Do things go wrong just when you are about to succeed?

d. Do you keep your anger bottled up?

e. Do you feel good when you feel bad?

f. Do you feel more noble than those who are just having fun in life?

6. a. Are your preoccupied with yourself?

b. Is your appearance the constant companion of your mind?

c. Do you find that you switch the conversation to yourself?

d. Do you feel diminished when someone else has the center of attention?

e. Do your mind games have only one voice—yours?

f. "Make my day. Tell me I'm wonderful." Does that sound like you?

7. Do you think:

a. What if, what if, what if?

b. I'll probably lose my job.

c. My date will probably reject me.

d. Sure, I got an "A" this time, but what will happen next time?

e. I could faint in the supermarket.

f. "Caution. Danger ahead." Could that be your motto?

8. a. Does nothing ever seem to go right?

b. Do you always seem to love someone who doesn't love you?

c. Is it easiest to make conversation when you are complaining?

d. Does it seem that there is no sense in going on?

e. Do you think you won't ever be happy?

f. Is your motto, "What a life!"?

9. a. Do your problems become permanent residents in your mind?

b. Are you irritated that others don't respect your careful planning?

c. "How can she have done that to me?" That was 6 months ago, and it still bugs you.

d. Should I or shouldn't I? Does it take terribly long to decide?

e. Do you long to be more perfect and have everything under control?

f. "To be or not to be?" Is that your question?

10. a. Do you spend a lot of time justifying yourself?

b. Do people tell you that you didn't answer the question?

c. Do you have a private inner life that no one should know about?

d. Are you considered a maverick, or a loner?

e. Do you prepare your excuses in advance?

f. "Keep your hands off me." Could that be your motto?

11. a. Do you often feel exploited?

b. Do you think you are a born loser?

c. Do you think you work harder than most everyone else?

    d. Do you rescue failure from the jaws of
       success?
    e. Do you do nothing when someone behind
       you talks throughout the movie?
    f. Does your sexual partner use you?

12. a. Do you think more about being loved than
       loving someone?
    b. Does your day center around getting
       compliments?
    c. Do people complain that you are self-
       centered?
    d. Do you become enraged when your faults
       are pointed out?
    e. Do you continue your single ways in a
       marriage?
    f. "Just mention my name." Is that a motto of
       yours?

After finishing the checklist, add the "trues" in
each group. If you found that your "trues" are widely
scattered, it probably indicates that your thinking is not
rigid, and consequently, the more flexible is your personality. Your negativity is probably mild, and you have
a large potential for growth.

If you had a large number of "trues" be careful not
to catch "psychology student's disease," which is the
belief that you have every problem and symptom in the
book. Most beginning psychology students get this
disease, but it is curable by further study.

If you found most of your answers concentrated in
a few categories, you have learned the value of *Listening
In.* You probably discovered some of your most common inner speeches. Those are the ones to watch for,
think about, and probably Stop and Switch. In one way

or other, all the thoughts in the checklist could be hurtful to you, and you will both think and feel better if you know your voice thoughts so intimately that you can change them the moment they pop up in your mind. *Knowing* your thoughts is the first step in *improving* them.

As we identify for you how we have grouped the various thoughts in the checklist, remember that this is not a test. Your answers will *not* "diagnose" your personality. It is simply a guide to help you Listen In.

CHECKLIST CATEGORIES

1 and 7 are Anxious/Phobic
2 and 8 are Depressive
3 and 9 are Obsessive
4 and 10 are Defensive/Detached
5 and 11 are Masochistic
6 and 12 are Narcissistic
The next chapters discuss them one at a time.

CHAPTER 11

THE ANXIOUS/PHOBIC THINKER
IT'S PANIC TIME

When a small child calls out to us at night that there's a monster in his room, we remain calm, turn on the light, and reassure him, because we know the monster is only in his imagination. We help him think differently, and that reassures him. Our fears change as we grow older, but they do not disappear. Sometimes those fears run wild and become an irrational and persistent dread. Then the fear is called a phobia.

If you're a phobic thinker, your mind is a welter of unreasonable fears, which deplete your energies and deprive you of enjoyment. Instead of thinking, "I'm really looking forward to the theater tonight," and setting yourself up for a good time, you think, "What will we do if we forget our tickets?" "What if there's no parking space?" "What if there's a fire and people all crowd for the exits?"

"What if somebody I had a fight with is at the party?"

145

"What if a cute guy comes on to me and I can't think of a thing to say?"

"What if the elevator gets stuck?"

More desperate scenarios may come to mind: "*What will I do if there's a gunman in the bank —*" This can lead to the ultimate *What ifs*. "What will happen to me if I go outside?" "What will happen if I get out of bed?" Focusing on fears (which is to think about fears) increases fear, and fears may build to phobias.

We can fill our minds around the clock with fears of muggings, collisions, dangerous storms, and hijackings that never materialize. Even if something does go wrong, it won't be made any better by our having agonized about it for hours in advance. Those were simply ineffectual thoughts with no value whatsoever. Those fears neither prevented nor solved the problem.

What they have done was hurt us in many ways. They deprived us of space for more productive thinking, caused us unnecessary suffering, and destroyed our enjoyment of life. Worst of all, they threaten to turn into full-fledged phobias which can contract and restrict our lives. We all know people who never leave their houses, or never fly, or can't be in a room with a dog, a cat, a bird, or a bug. How impoverished they are!

Has this scene ever happened to you? Has your thinking been *so weak* that you were unable to write a positive script? Or you were so consumed by an unremitting worry that you couldn't enjoy anything? Have you been so frightened by an imaginary fear that you were not able to prevent your own mind from racing ahead with scene after scene of every possible type of disaster?

The most common frightening mind script is, What Will I Do If—? What will I do if—

I can't think of anything to say?
the boat sinks?
the cable breaks?
I can't find a bathroom?
I lose my mind?

Underline the weakening word...*IF*.
Note that all these experiences follow a *programmed "if" script*—they occur in the mind of the scriptwriter. The internal speech creates elaborate enactments of disasters that are *painful*. The "if" is followed by a disaster. The pain is being created by the thinker who finishes his sentence with a catastrophe.

Since it is not helpful for you to produce sentences in your head that begin with an "if" and end with a tragedy, now is a time to think of a different ending for your "if" sentences.

"If I call Bill and ask him to have lunch with me, it could be fun catching up on the news."

"If I take a trip, I will see a lot of fascinating places."

"If I take the elevator, that will be faster and easier than climbing the stairs."

You can choose to end your sentences any way you wish. It just takes practice. Reorient your thinking away from your fears even *before* the fearful thought gets a chance to get started.

If you are afraid of elevators, choose not to think about the elevator when you are in it.

If you are afraid of crowds, or going out, try to

think of what you are going to do when you reach your destination. Concentrate on each minute detail.

When you are anxious, you are thinking that there is something dangerous that you are unable to manage successfully. When you are thinking at your best, you know that there are *few* things in life that are so dangerous that you won't be able to handle them safely. But if your thoughts of danger seem to be overwhelming you, Switch off that thought of danger.

Even if it is only an immediate Switch to reading a grocery list in your mind, if you can fill your Inner Speech with a less frightening subject, you will drive out the fear and eventually move to a more pleasant subject.

NANCY'S PHOBIA

Nancy was a professor at a university in New York. She was a high achiever, worked very hard, and probably worried more than was good for her. Yet, she was the last person that you would expect to have a phobia. She was successful at her work, had a wide circle of friends, and basically enjoyed her life. One winter weekend she was in the northern part of New Hampshire skiing with a friend, and driving back to New York on a Sunday night they were caught in a terrible blizzard called a white-out, because visibility is reduced to nearly zero. The road became impassable, and the highway patrol advised all cars to pull off the road. Nancy was able to get off the highway and about ten feet up into the driveway of an abandoned farmhouse. As the snow and the wind raged, Nancy and her friend did not dare to leave the car. They kept running the engine for brief periods so they could use the car's heater. But they did not leave the engine on for too long for fear that they would run out of gas and freeze.

About an hour after the sun came up, the storm quieted, and a snowplow came through and made the highway passable.

When Nancy returned to New York, she felt very shaken by the experience of being trapped in a dark, enclosed space, not knowing for sure where she was, and not knowing when, or even if, she would ever get out safely.

The following day when she was taking her usual subway ride to the university, she broke out in a cold sweat, her vision blurred, her heart beat so frantically she felt as if it would burst through her chest wall, she felt she was going to faint, she was dizzy, and she wondered if she was dying.

It was a full-blown panic attack, a severe attack of claustrophobia. Nancy had ridden that subway hundreds of times, and never felt anything like this before in her life—either in or out of a subway. She made her way out of the subway at the next stop, and got a taxi to the college. But it was about 100 blocks from her apartment, and she knew she could not afford that twice a day. At the same time, she did not dare risk getting into the subway alone again. She did manage it when she was with a friend, but that was not a practical solution for her phobia.

She tried psychotherapy, and found a therapist who could help her quiet her panic by direct attack on her phobic symptoms. Nancy was quick to see the relationship between being trapped in a car on a dark night, and being in a subway car in a dark subterranean tunnel. But knowing that did not dissolve the fear.

The method that helped her calm her fears, and
ride the subway successfully was to understand what
was going on in her Inner Speech. Her phobia began
when she was thinking neither about being trapped in
her car nor about the dark subway tunnel. But unwit-
tingly, something had caused her to trigger the fears
that she had felt during that long night of the blizzard.

It would have been *interesting* for Nancy and her
therapist to know exactly what the thought or memory
was that started the phobia; but it was not *necessary* to
do so in order for her to overcome her fears. She needed
prompt results, because her fears were upsetting, they
were beginning to affect other areas of her life, and the
phobia was expensive—two hundred blocks a day in a
taxi.

In her therapist's office she made a list of all the
things that she probably could think about in the subway which would frighten her: being alone in the midst
of strangers; all the doors were closed; when the train
stopped between stations, would it start again; the tunnel was dark; what would happen if there was a black-
out and all power was shut off, and they were led across
the third rail.

These were the thoughts she learned to Stop. She
practiced *Stopping* over and over again. Before long she
could Stop the thought by the time she had thought *the
first word* of any of her fears.

Then she practiced *Switching*. She prepared 10
pleasant, exciting, successful thoughts. She brought
reading material that would hold her attention. She discovered that reading a technical work in her professional field, biochemistry, did not divert her attention from
her fears. A suspenseful novel helped her Switch.

Then she Reoriented. She remembered her goals

and ambitions. She made a wish list, and kept adding to it as new ideas occurred to her. As she *reinforced her basic identity*, she strengthened her resolve to be rid of anything so sabotaging as a phobia.

With a mind filled with useful thoughts and Inner Speech Training techniques, she engaged a friend to ride the subway with her—but to sit across the aisle from her so she would be left alone to do her I.S.T. Then she had her friend sit at the other end of the car from her, and eventually in the next car. Then eventually she soloed, without a companion on the subway train with her. She was somewhat anxious. But she succeeded in riding all the way to the university, even though she had promised herself she could get off at any stop if the stress got too great for her.

The optimum therapy for Nancy was to help her develop her own set of thoughts and to be able to block out the thoughts that led to fears and phobias. One of the successful aspects of Inner Speech Training is that it enables a person to become his own therapist in a relatively short time. That in itself is a boost to one's self-confidence, and it provides another happy thought to Switch to, when overcoming an old fear.

Fears are in everyone. We start life about 20 inches long, 7 pounds of urges and appetites demanding satisfaction. We are helpless, and the rest of the world looms awesomely large. And so our fears begin.

The fears of infancy and childhood have been catalogued. The earliest fear is the loss of safety, especially the fear that arises from a sense of being dropped. A second fear at birth is of sudden loud noises. At eight months, the fear of strangers begins, followed swiftly by panic when separated from parents. By the time a child is a year old, the fear of physical injury is added to the list, and by age two, a child is thoughtful enough to have added fears of the dark, of large objects, and of changes in his familiar surroundings. The fear of animals arises at about age three, and threatening, mysterious, or supernatural creatures fearfully invade one's thoughts during the years six through eight. Growing intelligence after age nine allows one to become frightened of catastrophic events in the news, including one's own death. In preadolescence and adolescence, performance factors become fearsome, including fears of not being popular, of not succeeding in school, and the fear of sexual feelings and involvement.

Do those fears sound familiar to you? Well they may, because the same fears continue throughout life, staying basically the same while taking a somewhat more sophisticated shape. A loud truck in the street may not be frightening to an adult, but a sudden sonic boom will provoke thoughts of danger which will bring on that feeling of anxious dread.

The fear of abandonment, the fear of loss of love, and the fear of physical hurt are three fundamental fears that are thought to encompass all the specific fears that habitually, automatically, arise in our minds day after day.

The fears of childhood never are fully overcome; that is a fact of life. A goal of Inner Speech Training is to *recognize* fear, and not *deny* it. This is *Listening In*. It is important to *reflect* on the fear; this is *Underlining*. Processing what is going on in your mind will help you *evaluate* your fear.

Is it an accurate fear—exaggerated—childish—useful? Does the fear make sense? Will your fear lead you to better living? Slow it down. Does it do you any good?

JULIAN'S FEAR OF ABANDONMENT

Julian had a basic fear, one of those which has been there since infancy, and will show up in your mind all through your life. He had the fear of being alone, the fear of abandonment. He had these sentences occurring in his Inner Speech center: "I am alone. I am lonely. There is no one here for me. I don't know what I am going to do. Will it always be like this? I will probably spend my whole life alone. I am getting older. No one will want me."

What to do? Listen In. Identify the problem. The problem is that Julian thinks he is and will be alone. So far that is useful thinking because the problem has been pinpointed. What should be Underlined? Words like "no one," "always," "my whole life alone." Julian has now spent enough time dwelling on these thoughts. If he has begun to train his Inner Speech he will understand that it is not useful to keep those thoughts active in his mind. It is time to Switch. He knows the problem, and he knows he will depress himself if he dwells on the thought of being lonely, especially the thought that he will "always" be alone. Even the hardiest of personalities would become depressed if he were repetitiously to think that thought.

The task for Julian is to Switch immediately to any other thought. It is best to Switch to a thought that is pleasant, interesting, humorous, productive—anything to get off that abandonment theme as soon as possible.

Julian Switched to thinking about sports. If it was winter, he thought about basketball or boxing. If it was summer he Switched to baseball thoughts. That sounds like a superficial thing to do. But a pleasant, even though trivial thought, will be far more *helpful* to Julian

than thinking that he will be alone all his life. Whenever his abandonment fears entered his head, Julian
had a list of Switch thoughts.

Reorienting came next, and that meant solving the
problem of his loneliness by thinking, imaging, and visualizing himself as a person with friends, compan-
ions, and eventually, someone to love. This was a
longer-range project. He visualized a perfect day for
himself now, a year from now, 5 years from now. That
gave him a picture of his idealized self. He had a goal.
He imagined what he would like a biographer to write
about him. This gave him an idea about his basic values
in life, the kind of man he was, what he stood for. Then
he learned how to use a common time management
technique. Several times a day he would ask himself
how he could use the next few minutes to reach his goal
of not being lonely. This motivated him to pick up the
phone and chat for a few minutes. Other times he
would read a book on how to make conversation, or
photocopy diagrams of his family tree and send them
to all his cousins, or follow through on his plans to take
a course in assertiveness training. His Reorienting was
successful because he daydreamed what he wanted to
do, and then took sequential small practical steps to
become who he wanted to be, and go where he wanted
to go.

Julian had come by his fears of abandonment hon-
estly. There were good reasons in his life history for
him to have those fears, and they did not disappear
from his mind entirely. Late at night, or when he woke
up too early in the morning, or when he was very tired
and under great stress, those old familiar thoughts of
being alone would return. But a five-step I.S.T. program gave him the tools to overcome his fears, and he

felt very much better about himself when he found that he was not helpless in the face of those fears.

Fears can gain control of vital areas of your life. If your fears prevent you from carrying on your normal everyday activities, or if, in the opinion of the average person, you are living an inhibited life—then you need to give your fears special attention so they will not stay with you, or encroach on you even further for the rest of your life. How can you tell if your fears are serious enough to require special, perhaps professional attention? Here is how to answer that question. The serious fears are the ones that sabotage your productive work, that block you from receiving and giving love, and that interfere with having fun. You are seriously hurting yourself if you let those fears go without treatment.

The goal of Inner Speech Training is to help you make your fears manageable; to change self-defeating thoughts into useful ones; and give you better control of your life. With this kind of training, fears can be mastered.

CHAPTER 12

THE OBSESSIVE THINKER
HE LOVES ME, HE LOVES ME NOT

"Should I go?
—What if I don't?"

Do you hear your Inner Speech saying, "Should I or shouldn't I?" Double-talk—both sides of every question—verbal juggling.

The minds of obsessive thinkers are very busy places. Thoughts are always feverishly at work inside them but, unfortunately, they're the kind of thoughts that never get anywhere. They just keep going round and round, exhausting their thinker and accomplishing nothing. They're the embodiment of Henry David Thoreau's observation that "It is not enough to be busy—the question is: What are we busy *about*?"

THE CURIOUS CASE OF CATHY

Cathy had gone on a cruise two years before and had become involved with a member of the crew. He was French, charming, and Cathy had really fallen for him.

Unfortunately, he was also married, which Cathy knew, but which didn't have much reality for her since she never saw him in a domestic situation. As Cathy put it, "Totally, unexpectedly, I fell in love. I realized what was happening one night on board ship when I spent a totally sleepless night. I knew then it was love. I couldn't get my mind off him. I couldn't bear for him to be out of my sight. Amazing things happened. It was very good for me. I began to exercise every day. I lost five pounds. I stood erect, and I felt beautiful. I day-dreamed beautiful thoughts for hours at a time. I wanted to dance instead of walk. It was just good being alive. At the same time, I wondered what was happening to me. I felt I must be crazy. Was this the real Cathy? But I didn't care. I was ecstatic when I was with him. When I wasn't with him, he was on my mind constantly, and even my thoughts were infatuating."

After the cruise was over, the affair continued. Jacques' ship docked in New York on Tuesdays, and he and Cathy would meet at her apartment and spend the afternoon making love. She had told her boss a story about prolonged dental work and needing to take off Tuesday afternoons.

Cathy worried about the limitations of the affair. But she had a skilled lover and she daydreamed of the time when they would be together more. At least she was sure she would keep seeing him Tuesday afternoons. But one day Jacques' ship was assigned to a new route, and the New York stops ended. Some painful thoughts began to creep into Cathy's mind.

A couple of weeks went by without any word from him, and she began to think about Jacques even more. There must have been some mistake. Did the mail get lost? Could he have mislaid her phone number?

The longer Cathy didn't hear from Jacques, the more strongly she heard her obsessive voices. "He'll call. I know he misses me." "He's got to call. I won't be able to stand it if he doesn't." Cathy's obsession nearly took over her life. It was a torment, with that voice at her every moment. "Suppose he calls and you are not here." Cathy knew she was contributing to her own suffering, but she seemed powerless to let go of her obsession. She clung to it because it was her *only link* with Jacques.

Gradually, as she talked about Jacques in her therapy sessions, she recognized that her hidden thoughts about him were filled with rage at him for what he had done to her. Cathy finally heard her own angry voice. She was furious at Jacques. She imagined a confrontation. She wrote a scenario in her head in which the telephone rang—in her head, of course. It was Jacques calling her back after the 6 months that had gone by since the cruise. Cathy took a deep breath and said to him, "Shove it. I don't care if your ship sank. Get lost, low life."

That was the voice that broke the spell. After she practiced that inner speech about fifty times, usually out loud, with plenty of feeling, she emerged from her obsessive thinking. She began to reclaim her mind, and herself. The power she had *given to Jacques* at last had returned to the place it belonged—inside her own head in her own inner speech center.

BEING STUCK

Every day, millions of people wake up in a jail—prisoners of their own thoughts. If you're one of these

people, you wake up each morning to the same dialogue you woke up to yesterday morning—and the day
before. Your thoughts are repetitive, inconclusive, and
usually useless. Obsessive thoughts don't move you
forward, and you know it; yet you can't seem to stop.

No matter how many times you ask yourself, "Why
doesn't he call? He *said* he'd call," the phone is unlikely
to ring. The answer to your question and the power to
pick up the phone are in *his* head, not yours, and you
can't put yourself into somebody else's head. What you
need to do instead is redirect your thinking to its
proper province: your *own* head.

Once you do that, you're on your way to freedom.
You'll be able to get to the root of your obsessions by
sorting out and expressing your true emotions.

Not all obsessions are without value. Many of the
great moments of mankind have been due to a particular obsession, ranging from great scientific discoveries
like radium to the building of castles and cathedrals
that took centuries to complete. Much of our great literature is concerned with obsessiveness, ranging from
Madame Bovary's erotic preoccupations to the pursuit of
the White Whale *Moby-Dick*. Many of the major charac-
ters in the fictional landscapes are governed and ruled
by passions or obsessions, whether they be the immor-
tal *Don Quixote* on his endless quest or the simple lust-
ing of more modern Candides.

Almost all professional people are highly obsessive in their thinking. They have to be—to survive in
working their way through professional training and,
later, to retain good work habits which are often, by
necessity, meticulous, repetitive, and dogged: what
Freud ironically called—lining out the scientific
method—"our poor patchy attempts."

Who would want to go to a doctor who did not make a *complete* inquiry about all the related symptoms, or to an attorney who neglected to incorporate *all* the relevant facts in preparing a case? Obsessive style serves us well in developing good school and work habits. The well-prepared homemaker should be a bit obsessive if she or he is going to do all of the necessary work effectively. The hidden clue here is, "What is all of the *necessary* work?" The obsessive thinker often can't decide.

Unfortunately, the obsessive style may also lead to constant undesirable thoughts that intrude painfully and control the inner speech. Obsessive thoughts come to dominate the normal necessary flow of more important and related thinking. Special thoughts and preoccupations lead to the development of obsessive inner speech, and the person is so programmed to think in a certain way that he becomes a prisoner of his own mind.

How do you recognize the harmless obsession that troubles your thinking? Focus on the following criteria. Keep in mind that there is much ambiguity about establishing a judgment of where a productive positive thought ends and where an obsessive thought begins.

Obsessive thinking is *harmful* when:

1. There is great *repetition* and *waste* in the recurring thought.
2. It represents an *overreaction*.
3. The overreaction is particularly *painful* and accompanied by a feeling of *anxious dread*.
4. The thinker realizes that basically the thought is "*useless*."
5. The thinking has a routinely *oppositional* quality ("You say 'yes,' I say 'no' ").

6. The thoughts are filled with strong personal needs for perfection and control.

Thinking that is not obsessional maintains *flexibility* and *internal freedom* to adapt freshly to each new situation instead of repeating the same old response.

As soon as you recognize that the nature of the obsession is really a destructive voice, you can begin to STOP the voice and work on *Switching*.

"This voice really doesn't do me any good. I can tune in on a more helpful voice."

List your three most demanding obsessions. Practice *Stopping* each thought.

1. _____
2. _____
3. _____

The Stop and Switch techniques are the fastest and most effective techniques there are for the relief of obsessions. Obsessive thinking can go on almost endlessly — if you let it alone.

CHAPTER 13

THE NARCISSISTIC THINKER
ME, MYSELF, AND I

Some recorders of the world scene have dubbed our present era "The Age of Narcissism." Evidence of it is found in phrases like "the Me Generation" and "looking out for Number One."

Narcissists are preoccupied with their own needs, wishes, desires, appetites, ambitions, pleasures, and comforts, to the exclusion of anyone else's. They usually don't see anything wrong with their behavior, since it's certainly pleasant to have your own way in everything. The people we usually see in treatment are the ones who have to deal with narcissists in close relationships: and a more baffled, frustrated, exasperated group probably doesn't exist.

We hear laments like, "He hardly knows I'm alive"; "Not once has she ever asked what kind of day I've had"; "In six years of marriage I've never picked out a movie." What the troubled spouse or friend doesn't understand is that the first sentence is all too true. The narcissist *doesn't* know anyone else is alive. Other people are allowed to exist only if they worship the narcissist.

A narcissist is like a person with a hammering toothache. He's so consumed by his inner distress he has no room for other considerations. His self-centeredness is a device built to protect him from uncertainties about himself. Over the years, it becomes impenetrable, allowing no room for outside voices. You know you're dealing with a narcissist when your own practical, social, and sexual needs are ruthlessly and consistently ignored.

There are all levels of narcissism, of course, and all of us have it to some degree. You can check to see if yours is turning into a problem by asking yourself some questions: "Am I overly absorbed with myself?" "Do people I deal with get annoyed a lot?" "Does my family feel neglected?" "Have people frequently called me selfish?"

Contented narcissists may not see much reason to change; but experience demonstrates forcefully that narcissists eventually pay for their selfishness. Without noticing what they're doing, they drive people away until they begin to feel the pain of uninvolved loneliness and a hollow life.

Narcissism occurs when a person hears only his own voice. If this appears contrary to what was urged about listening to your own voice as much as possible, note a difference here, because the distinction is critical. It is very important to be sensitive to the voices of other people as well as to one's own. If a person doesn't consider what other people might be experiencing internally, and cannot appreciate others' feelings, then a narcissistic condition may exist.

A narcissist is someone who finishes a long monologue about himself and then says to his partner:

"Now let's talk about *you*. How do you like my
new suit?"

WHAT DOES THIS MEAN TO YOU?

It means that in choosing friends, dates, and
lovers, you should consider how well the other person
relates to you. Is he or she heavily narcissistic?

Do they relate to your ideas? Do your wishes matter to them?

Frequently, people come for therapy with a particular problem, which is a variation of this same theme.
Why can't I get along with T? T may be a friend—
lover—coworker—relative.

The reason may be that the person has failed to
realize the extent that *narcissism* has controlled the
relationship.

THE NARCISSIST'S INTERNAL DIALOGUES ARE MOST APT TO BE MONOLOGUES

See if you can recognize the source of difficulty in
this problem:

Karen R. was crushed. She was a highly responsible person, and felt defeated when she came in for
therapy with a failing marriage. She described her hus-

band Ken as a charmer, a devastatingly good-looking guy who dressed to the nines. He was successful at work but neglected Karen. He would go out most evenings, and played golf the entire weekend, leaving her alone at home with the children. Eventually, Karen came to learn the sad truth that Ken could deny others everything and refuse himself nothing.

Ken didn't seem to feel embarrassed about leaving his wife and children alone all weekend, plus several nights a week. The real problem didn't emerge until a complete history had been taken.

Ken, who reluctantly agreed to try marriage counseling, admitted that he never heard Karen's voice in his head. In fact, he never heard anyone else's voice in his head. His internal speech was a preoccupation with his needs, wants, desires, wishes, appetites, ambitions, pleasures. Unfortunately, as a narcissistic personality, Ken had no interest in changing. He didn't see anything wrong with his thinking. Fortunately, however, Karen did. She saw there was reality in her belief that he never considered her needs, and that she didn't exist for him.

Narcissists, usually after some painful reversal in life, can learn that others also have their own inner speech. Unlikely as it seems from the outside, narcissists live painful inner lives. A wounded, motivated narcissist can change, one tiny step at a time. First, he needs to Listen In and hear his own words about his own emptiness—which has often prompted him to compensate by saying, "I just made it with three gorgeous women, aren't I the jock?" The narcissist can hear that his inner voice is full of himself, and it hasn't made him happy. "Listen In and Underline." Tell that to a narcissist and he will find that he has only heard his own needs, his own voice, and his own desperate longing for attention.

Through *Reorienting*, a narcissist can, with a will to change, discover other thoughts, other voices, and then a richer world.

TREVOR'S CASE

Trevor was an elegant-looking man with a grandiose sense of his own importance. Three wives had divorced him, but there were always other women at hand ready to bask in his charisma. He had alienated his children from two of his marriages. His children found that being in his presence was like being in the theater watching a master showman. But just like being in the theater, there was hardly any direct interaction between the actor and the audience. Their father only wanted the children to laugh and applaud, never to be part of the act.

After three divorces, Trevor came to realize that he had no close friends. Everyone seemed to want him at a cocktail party, but no one wanted to spend a weekend or a vacation with him—at least not if they had known him for more than 6 months.

Trevor was spending more and more time alone, and it came to be depressing for him. He was psychologically addicted to attention, but he was finding that being noticed by others was beginning to mean less and less to him. He began to notice that he couldn't stand being alone for more than a couple of hours. After that he would want to be with someone, but found it unsatisfying because he resented having to make the effort to impress someone, and he often despised the people he would choose to impress.

Finally a college classmate, whom he had known
for 30 years, had the courage to level with Trevor. He
told Trevor that he was suffering from more than a mid-
life crisis, more than the 20-year itch. His friend described the condition as a deep inner emptiness, which
Trevor had tried to fill with women, cars, boats, and
fitness. None of it had filled the hunger and longing he
had for self-respect and self-love.

Trevor did not react kindly to this appraisal of himself. He never had been able to take criticism, and this
had cut deeply and he tried to push it away. But he was
highly intelligent, and typically, he thought he could
help himself better than anyone else would be able to.
He read articles and books about narcissism, and ar-
rived at his own conclusion that he would try therapy.
His motivation at that time was to become *more* perfect,
more powerful, more sought-after. He thought therapy
would help him to become the most successful narcissist in the world. Therefore, he tried to find the greatest
psychoanalyst in the world so that he would be the
patient.

Therapy did not go the way that Trevor expected.
He quickly became enraged at the analyst, who confronted Trevor's inner emptiness, and interpreted his
desperate attempts to fill it with notoriety. Two therapists later, Trevor found himself trying Inner Speech
Therapy. That was not uneventful either; but his earlier
therapies had at least softened him up a bit to listen to
someone besides himself. He was able to listen to his
new therapist, who told him the goal of therapy was
not to become more perfect, but to become more
human.

The first step in I.S.T. for him, of course, was to
Listen In. When Trevor tried to Listen In, he only heard

that he was the greatest, the handsomest, the best lover, the most brilliant, most gifted. But was there another inner voice under the voice of bravado? Trevor listened and listened, and began to hear it. He heard, underneath, that he had woefully little self-esteem. He thought he was superficial, that he had never been able to love anyone, and had never been able to know another person deeply because he could not empathize with another person's feelings.

This first step in therapy was depressing, even frightening, for Trevor. But here his old belief that he knew best helped him out. His therapist taught him the outline of how to proceed with Inner Speech Therapy, and Trevor set out to outdistance the therapist. He came into each session with new insights based on his own use and adaptation of the five steps of I.S.T. The painful insight into his condition alternately made him want to give up, or revert back to impressing yet another desirable woman. But eventually he pushed on to find an end to the meaninglessness he had always felt in his life.

Listening In and *Underlining* were so painful for Trevor that he was an apt student of *Stopping* and *Switching*. But he had little experience in *Switching* to anything but narcissistic grandiosity. He then decided, on his own, of course, that he would make an academic study of empathy. Perhaps this would be powerful enough to draw him away from narcissistic thoughts. This proved to be the tactic that enabled him to Reorient. For longer and longer periods he was able to enjoy the fulfillment that came from knowing another person deeply. When he learned to give unselfishly more and more, he began to respect and, eventually, *like* himself—and others. He tried the same tactic in his work. Rather than going for the quick fix and the flashy show, he found it fascinating to begin to study something in depth.

Now when Trevor sees his name in lights in his fantasy world, he has an automatic thought that goes Stop, Switch, Reorient.

CHAPTER 14

THE MASOCHISTIC THINKER
THE PLEASURE OF PAIN

"Who, me? Want to suffer?"

That's what everybody says; but the truth, in many cases, is just the opposite. There are persons who actually cherish Murphy's law and secretly hope that anything that can go wrong will go wrong.

Ralph Waldo Emerson said, "There are people who have an appetite for grief." Many otherwise intelligent human beings have set themselves up to suffer to some degree or other. Some are mild practitioners of this ultimately self-defeating type of thinking; others carry it to extremes. Masochism ranges in severity from not allowing one's self to succeed to actually enjoying pain. And there are stops all along the way.

The masochistic thinker is one who confuses weakness with strength, who attempts to control others by manipulating others by his suffering. Masochists are self-critical and loaded with self-imposed guilt, most of it with little basis in common sense. If you dig far enough back, you're more than likely to find a "put-down" parent whose words and attitudes the person internalized as a child. The masochistic child learned that he could keep himself safe in the family by putting himself down, or at least not thinking and acting in a way that indicated that he was happy and successful. His basic thought about himself became the belief that he was guilty and unworthy. The natural result of his sense of himself was that pain and suffering was his lot in life.

The next time you compliment a woman on her dress, notice whether or not she replies with something like, "This old bag is fifteen years old," or "Blue's not my color but it was on sale."

We do not know what thought this woman might have had between your compliment and her apologetic response. Perhaps Marcia's discovery sheds light on the need to apologize.

Marcia discovered during I.S.T. that her "in-between thought" after a compliment was "I'm not really attractive." And then when she Listened In even more carefully she found another thought that she recognized had been there since childhood. It was, "I am not supposed to think I am pretty. *That* is 'vain.' "

It is no wonder that Marcia felt uneasy whenever she was complimented, because a compliment was always paired in her mind with a parallel thought of how *vain* it was for her to look nice.

Most people have gone through life never paying attention to this stream of thinking that underlies and *determines the feeling*. People most often feel the *feeling* without connecting it to the cause of the feeling. Marcia was programmed to apologize for herself when complimented, and she did not consciously know why until she discovered the hidden power of her hidden speech.

Unfortunately, this thinking pattern can become solidly entrenched. The sufferer doesn't think himself worthy of happiness and puts obstacles in the way whenever good times threaten to come too close. The thinking goes something like this: "It's a beautiful day—perfect for the tennis matches. But the house is a mess (or the lawn needs mowing). I'd better stay home and take care of it." This is followed by a deep sigh and a surreptitious feeling of nobility. "See how *good* I am," it proclaims. "*I* don't fritter away my time. You go to the tennis matches and enjoy yourself!" Whether the other person goes or stays, the day has been ruined. The masochist, beginning with his own guilt, has successfully passed on his guilt to others.

Masochistic thinking exacts a terrible toll on both the masochist and those around him. The masochist thinks he is not entitled. He then is annoyed with others who do enjoy life. When masochism can be understood and stopped as it originates, one's self-esteem will rise; injustice-collecting will diminish; "punishments" will be replaced by rewards. After all, if we think about it, we know there are better ways to get pleasure than by feeling pathetic and sorry for ourselves.

HOW MUCH MASOCHISM IS IN YOUR THINKING?

Do you wash the dishes alone in the kitchen while the rest of the family is watching the Superbowl?

Do you chronically feel sorry for yourself?

Do you get turned on sexually by seeing yourself put down?

If you are suffering in any way, *the burden of proof is on you to prove that you haven't brought it on yourself.*

We recognize that there is enormous innocent suffering because of discrimination, poverty, war, physical and mental handicaps—just getting bad breaks through the accidents of living.

We are aware that there are self-centered and simplistic self-help writings that ignore the complexities of the problems in the world. Such real problems cannot be wished away by just thinking happy thoughts. We offer the Inner Speech Training procedures in order for any person to be more effective in the quest for social betterment. The means to eliminate needless fears and discouragement brought on by depressogenic thinking can lead to more successful thinking, and thus to greater emotional and physical stamina. Effective reformers do not come from the ranks of the completely downtrodden thinkers. The battering imposed on oneself by chronically depressed or masochistic thinking will probably make it impossible for such thinkers to contribute to the betterment of society. I.S.T. is a means of avoiding the pitfalls of that weak thinking.

Therefore, for present purposes, when thinking about *yourself*, it is best to disregard the unfortunate and unfair accidents of your history. You are ultimately responsible now for the trend of the thoughts in your mind. When thinking now about your own thinking, your time is best spent in finding the answer to this question: "What voices am I hearing in my inner speech?"

Masochists start their inner speech by thinking:

"Happiness is impossible."

THEREFORE, MASOCHISTS—

Prove to themselves that the world is not a happy place by anticipating and then provoking rejection and disappointment. They become angry that they were treated this way, feeling sorry for themselves. Masochists collect injustices. They savor a sweet sadness as they prove to themselves that the world is no damn good. They know suffering. They expect it. Masochists go on weak-thinking:

> "I am *safer* if I put myself down. If I beat them to it, nobody else can do it."

THEREFORE, MASOCHISTS—

Anticipate and expect criticism, even imagine it when criticism may not be there. Their own self-criticism beats others to the punch. They use about half their mental energy preparing for criticism. They capitulate (and give indications of weakness) as a way of life with spouse, boss, neighbors, and friends.

Masochistic Self-Defeating Thinking runs:

> "I think people will take better care of me if I suffer (i.e., don't do well)."

THEREFORE, MASOCHISTS—

Provoke guilt in other people by playing the martyr. The masochist says, "I didn't do well." The other per-

son thinks: "Then I must not have done well either."
The masochist inflicts pain on others.

MASOCHISTIC RUSS

Russ fit the stereotype so completely that it almost
seemed he had studied books on masochism so he
could imitate all the traits that ma‾ ‾hists were known
to have. He even had the same s, ‾ptom as novelist
Leopold von Sacher-Masoch—from whom the term was
derived: Russ also wished that his wife would be un-
faithful to him, and provoked it in strange ways, as
Sacher-Masoch had done in the nineteenth century.

Russ was born a few months after his father had
died. His mother was depressed and under great stress.
He learned early to feel guilty for his existence, because
he felt he was the cause of his mother's imprisonment in
a life of drudgery. When Russ was four his mother re-
married. Her second husband was much older, with
four grown children. Russ again felt an unwanted
child. To keep her new husband happy, Russ's mother
spent as little time with Russ as possible. Any trouble
he caused gave rise to rage on the part of both his
parents.

Russ grew into a quiet, compliant boy who tried
always to be pleasant and ingratiating. He tried never to
put himself forward, nor to call any attention to himself. As a child, he literally had felt that his life would
be in danger if he stood out in any way. The rage he felt
inwardly at being constantly mistreated was buried so
deeply he rarely experienced it. But occasionally he
would have dreams of destroying the world, followed at
once by a scene in which he was tortured.

The roots of his masochism are classic. Given those early experiences when his personality was being formed, he could scarcely have turned out any other way. When he was nearly 40 he married a dominating woman much older than himself. After 2 years of marriage, she grew so angry at his helpless masochism that she threatened him with divorce unless he sought therapy.

Where should the therapy begin? The answer to that was easy. It could begin with practically any thought that came into Russ's mind. His thoughts were filled with one message, "Don't make waves." His masochistic life-style was being reinforced minute-by-minute as he thought, "I will be in danger if I am assertive, or outstanding, or intelligent, or act in any way as if I am entitled to anything at all."

Inner Speech Training could have been very prolonged and difficult for Russ except for the fact that he had an extremely high I.Q., and he was eager to please any person in authority, including, in this situation, his therapist. His rage at anyone in positions of power or prominence was explored with him, so he could understand at last he had someone who wanted him to stand up for himself rather than be a doormat. His therapist and he had a good working relationship.

Listening In came slowly, because most of his put-down thoughts were so automatic that he did not attend to them. In time he heard his inner voice, and Underlined what he called his philosophy of life: to be nonexistent. His words were "Don't speak first, don't offer a suggestion; people don't like me, get away from others as soon as I can before I make a mistake and get thrown out"; and so on.

Russ found it difficult to Switch at first, because

his habits of martyrdom were so ingrained that he could scarcely conceive of any other way to think of himself or his life. He thought at age 42 he would never be able to Switch. But here he found the five-step program of I.S.T. particularly helpful because it gave him a *formula* that he could *follow*. He only had to learn how to fill in the blanks, 1, 2, 3, 4, 5. This he did, and the progress, after many repetitions, became nearly automatic. He was a C.P.A., and accustomed to following set accounting principles. He finally found it easy to change his thinking by a formula he could understand.

The most difficult inner thought for Russ was that he would be in great danger if he did not allow himself to get walked on. The classic theory of masochism is that one thinks one will be castrated if he seeks pleasure. To uproot the roots of his masochism he practiced saying sentences of entitlement: everything from, "I would like a glass of water" in a restaurant, to "I want to make love with you, Marie," when with his wife. The old automatic thought was that he would be rejected. In the presence of his therapist he could examine that thought more realistically, and recognize that the request was reasonable and apt to be met with a positive response. And, he realized, even when the answer was no, he could continue the discussion and find some satisfying options.

After practicing different thoughts, he was able to translate his thoughts into behavior. Naturally, his anxiety would rise on those occasions but, with increasing success, he felt less guilty about his needs and wishes, and more entitled to take the next step of seeing himself as a human being with the same rights as other humans in the world.

Ten years after his therapy concluded, he wrote a

Christmas card to his therapist on which he said, "I'm still throwing off the shackles of the past. I hardly ever hear that old voice that used to say, 'I'm worthless, I can't make it.' The sentence I most often hear now is, 'I am going to do some of the things I want.' Life seems good. I'm enjoying it."

Listen In. Do you feel sorry for yourself in those private inner speeches that only you can hear? And can you admit to yourself that it makes you feel a little special that you are such a self-sacrificing martyr? STOP. Why? Because your thoughts lead you on to more defeat and suffering. You are rewarding yourself for suffering. If you reward yourself for it, you will seek out more suffering. Is that really what you want in life?

Listen In and Stop the masochistic thought right at the beginning. The weak thought yields the painful feeling. Underline it and Reorient your thinking to those experiences where pain is not the primary pleasure.

CHAPTER 15

THE DEPRESSIVE THINKER
THINKING THE WORST

We're all sad from time to time. When we confront the death of a loved one, the end of a romance, the loss of a job, or even a major disappointment, we're bound to be sad. That's part of the human condition.

But when sadness is *self*-generated and becomes a *constant companion*, psychology calls it by another name: *Depression*. The most common personality problem in our culture is depressive thinking. To a depressed person, sadness is a way of life. The outlook is always gloomy. Depression saps your strength, eliminates your enthusiasm, and turns life into misery. At its most extreme, it reduces the sufferer to despair and thoughts of suicide.

There's a vital difference between a legitimate sadness and depressive thinking. The former is always related to a genuine distress. Something real, usually some loss, has happened, and it has happened recently. On the other hand, the person who is lamenting a lost love 5, perhaps even 20, years after the event, has been nurturing depressive thoughts. Rooted in a painful loss of self-esteem, this type of thinking overplays self-blame. "He didn't love me, which only goes to prove I'm not lovable" is the thought about yourself that comes to mind and, worse, stays there.

Thinking your way up from depression begins with sizing up your thinking about your life. What is your sense of your self in the world, and how do you manage yourself in it?

Your beliefs about yourself and your beliefs about how you manage your world contain the key to your sense of self. Those beliefs are worth examining, at least daily. There are certain thoughts that lead to competence and confidence. The thinking of competent people has been subjected to careful research, and how they think can be practiced and learned by everyone—if not perfectly, certainly with considerable success.

Some thoughts about yourself can and do lead to stress and powerlessness, in great contrast to the thinking that leads to confidence. For example, whenever you are thinking that the outcome of some event in your life will be negative, you are almost surely going to depress yourself.

Thought has had little systematic psychological study until recently. The latest research has centered on both *how* to think and *what* to think. It is now known *what* thoughts lead to emotional disorders. As a result, Inner Speech Training is able to describe those destructive thoughts in detail. How to change those thoughts can now be taught by a systematic process that shortens both the degree and the duration of emotional suffering.

It all starts with your thoughts about yourself. What are your thoughts about yourself?

If you categorized your thinking as depressed when you finished the checklist, then you know the overwhelming feelings of helplessness that kind of thinking produces. You think nothing excites you. You think you are bored. You think your prospects look bleak. You think you will never lose weight. You think you will always be incompetent. You think nothing will make any difference.

Experience has shown that depression responds dramatically to a restructuring of one's thoughts. Pick out the destructive words in the last paragraph: "Never." "Always." "Nothing." Those are the villains in the piece, the universalizations that bind you. They fortify your feelings of helplessness and impair your power to function. If things will *never* be right, why try?

Depressed people are the victims of distorted thinking. The depressed person accentuates the negative, eliminating the positive. Thus, they see their environment as barren and themselves as a container of shortcomings.

Fortunately, that kind of thinking can be stopped.

LIVING WITH DEPRESSING VOICES

The story is told of the man who came to see the psychiatrist, complaining of depression. "What's the trouble?" asked the doctor.

"Well, two months ago my grandfather died and left me $75,000. One month ago, a distant cousin died and left me $100,000."

"So why are you depressed?"

"This month, *nothing!*"

Depressed people will find *something*, anything to *think* about that will depress them.

Are there heavy, serious voices meeting constantly in your mental space, filling your head with ideas that cause you to feel *blue* or *sad?*—Heavy voices packed with *weakening* words and stopping you from experiencing more powerful thinking?

Are you able to connect these negative feelings about yourself and your world with recurring patterns of negative thoughts? If you Listen In, you will notice most of these repetitive negative statements about yourself are connected to a *preceding automatic thought*— a thought that enters your mental space without deliberate conscious selection.

More and more attention has been paid recently to the fact that we develop *automatic voices* even when we don't want them. Since they appear so readily, they seem to be automatic. But, in fact, they can be stopped. The negative feelings associated with the inner voices can be prevented.

Randolph felt uneasy whenever the TV weather announcer predicted that the next day would be a beautiful one. After he did some detective work on his thinking, he learned that "beautiful day tomorrow" brought on an immediate response in his thinking of "a nice day makes demands on me." What demands? Randolph was a loner, and a nice day made him feel guilty, because so many people had told him that he should be out making the most of his day: looking for a job, meeting a friend, going to the beach. As he Listened In further, he heard his inner speech becoming angry at his therapist. He had become uncomfortable about his therapy recently, and *Listening In* and *Underlining* uncovered his thought that the therapist would expect him to be more active and get more involved in life. And worse, he thought his therapist regarded him as a failure in therapy, and disliked him for his slow progress.

When Randolph marshaled these thoughts which he said just "popped into his mind," he could then look at them and discuss them more sensibly. He came to realize why he automatically "felt" badly about the prospect of good weather, and why he "felt" badly about coming to therapy. Once he knew that his feelings came from certain thoughts, he was able to do something about those thoughts.

The hidden power of his hidden inner speech was no longer hidden after he learned how to search for those automatic thoughts. The thoughts were not useful nor true, and he changed them. At that point he was able to control his feelings.

It is important in dealing with the unwanted and unjustified voices that keep causing depression to match the "down" feeling with the negative thoughts that precede it.

Keep a record. Every time you feel "blue," what is the thought behind it? Is that thought so necessary that you *have* to have it? Or would you be better off without it?

Consider the thought. What makes it so automatic? You may still think you have no voluntary control over those so-called automatic thoughts. But you can control your own mind. Is it vital to your existence to have that thought and feel bad? You can decide what to think.

Build a bridge to more positive self-esteem by learning how to deal with your own inner voice on more realistic terms. The first step is to rid yourself of the persisting negative voices in your head.

To become depressed beyond ordinary temporary sadness at a life event involves three different thinking distortions: distorting the view of your past, your present, and your future.

1. DEPRESSED PERSONS DISTORT WHAT THEY SEE (PRESENT)

Persons who chronically get "down" interpret the environment in a distorted pessimistic way to draw the maximum negative feelings into their mind.

There are several common ways that depressed people do this: They pick up mainly negative messages from their world. If it rains, they dwell on those aspects of the day that are interrupted. "It only rains when I have something special to do." "Why does the teacher *sigh only* at me?"

They have not learned to control the automatic thoughts that put themselves in jeopardy. They undo a happy thought almost as soon as it appears. "I enjoyed the Michael Jackson concert. I'll never have a glamorous career like that."

2. DEPRESSED PERSONS DISTORT THEIR OWN HISTORY (PAST)

Depressed persons can spot their faults like a scientist looking through a microscope.

They magnify their own past failures.

Their self-worth is in the state of a perpetual bear

market—falling, falling. No ability or achievement, however publicly acclaimed, is acceptable evidence of either their worth or talent. They have six plausible inner thoughts and ready excuses for why they didn't merit any good thing in their lives. "I think I just knew how to fool people." In severe depression, a person may think, "I should never have been born."

3. DEPRESSED PERSONS DISTORT THEIR FUTURE CHANCES (FUTURE)

They believe things will get worse for them.
They have been predicting a crash in their well-being for years. They will flunk the test, lose their job, be overwhelmed by life, end up needing round-the-clock nursing care. A cure for cancer may someday be discovered, but they think it will come only after they are dead. "Things are bad now, but the worst is yet to come."

These thoughts are examples of people overresponding to thoughts going on in their heads. These off-target thoughts divert the thinker from certain important data about themselves. *All three distortions lead to a dominating inner weakness.*

How many times have you overlooked positive traits in yourself to search out the negative ones when you are feeling low? Negative statements about you prevail, especially when you are already down.

"You don't understand. Things really are bad
for me. It won't work out."

You have heard the story of the man who went to

see a psychologist because he felt he had an inferiority complex. After interviews and tests the psychologist told him, "You don't have an inferiority *complex*. You are *truly* inferior."

An apocryphal story, we hope, but it raises an important issue for the study of Inner Speech Training. What if you are pessimistic for good reasons—that is, you are completely *realistic* in expecting that you will fail at something? Should you be Pollyanna and deny reality? The answer is no. I.S.T. calls for truthful and accurate thinking. It can be useful to think negatively when it is factually negative. Negative thinking is an early phase in self-improvement. It provides an analysis of the problem so that a plan for productive thinking can begin.

A bad situation is made worse by thinking dominated by fright and helplessness. When panic and despair take over, the mind becomes woefully inefficient. Haven't you been almost unable to say your own name when you were acutely anxious? It is this kind of thinking that needs to be Stopped and Switched.

There is scarcely anyone who cannot better his or her own life. However bleak things are, virtually anyone can cope with the world more successfully with a thinking style that reduces the focus on discouragement and worry, and instead provides a means to be more relaxed and efficient in one's thinking. The negative thought is worth *Listening In* to, and it helps to gripe and let off some steam (up to a point). But getting it off your chest is only the preliminary exercise. The next thing is to Switch to productive and problem-solving thinking. As the Scottish poem goes, "I'll lay meself down and bleed awhile, and rise and fight again."

When negative thinking is allowed to become habitual it becomes depressogenic (depression-causing) thinking.

Listen In and start to repattern your negative thinking.

Ferret out the automatic thought that exists as a voice in your head, and occurs behind every negative feeling.

It takes work to become aware and connect the feeling with the thought that existed *immediately* before it. You will change your feeling when you become more aware of the *automatic thought* that caused the feeling in the first place.

Use the following checklist of feelings as a start in identifying those *feelings* that flow from depressogenic *thinking*.

How often do you have each of the following symptoms?

	Never	Some-times	Fre-quently	All the time
1. Feel sad, blue/ down	___	___	___	___
2. Feel lack of satisfaction in most things	___	___	___	___
3. Feel lonely	___	___	___	___
4. Feel bored/ little interest in most things	___	___	___	___
5. Decline in sexual interest or pleasure	___	___	___	___

6. Trouble falling asleep or staying asleep   ___   ___   ___   ___
7. Poor appetite   ___   ___   ___   ___
8. Cry easily or feel like crying   ___   ___   ___   ___
9. Little or no energy   ___   ___   ___   ___
10. Easily fatigued   ___   ___   ___   ___
11. Feeling hopeless   ___   ___   ___   ___
12. Feeling slowed down   ___   ___   ___   ___
13. Blame yourself, overly self-critical   ___   ___   ___   ___
14. Withdrawn   ___   ___   ___   ___
15. Increasingly indecisive, unable to act   ___   ___   ___   ___
16. Suicidal feelings and preoccupations   ___   ___   ___   ___
17. Worried   ___   ___   ___   ___
18. Overly preoccupied about minutiae   ___   ___   ___   ___
19. Feeling of disappointment and disgust with oneself   ___   ___   ___   ___

20. Have trouble
    making plans   _____   _____   _____   _____

WHAT ARE THE CHARACTERISTICS OF THESE DEPRESSIVE THOUGHTS?

In content. These thoughts overreflect the dejected mood persuasively. The common themes are worthlessness, hopelessness, pessimism, and despair.

Depressed persons take their suffering very *seriously.* They are unable to see that frequently there is a selected focus on the negative in the environment. They feel so bad that they ignore any evidence that will relieve their pessimism and cheer them up. They block out ideas that will disturb their relentless pessimism.

In structure. Starting with false premises, depressed persons draw false conclusions.

Look at these depressive sentences again. Underline all the overly negative generalizations.

"What's the use—nothing ever goes right."

Underline *nothing.*
Is it really true that nothing goes right, or have you structured your thinking so that you are going to make yourself feel that way? Try this sentence:

"I just can't cope with anything."

Underline *anything.*
Is it true; or is it again a tendency to overgeneralize in such a fashion that you feel bad because of an *exaggerated* conclusion?

Depressed people are constantly "setting up" negative circumstances to prove their worthlessness, and the hopelessness of the situation. For instance, they commonly withdraw and isolate themselves. Then they use the withdrawal to prove that:

> "No one likes or cares for me. How could they? I'm no fun."

Or they *focus on an irrelevant aspect of a problem*, such as ruminating in a guilty way:

> If *only I had*—
> "—raised my children differently—"
> "—bought that IBM stock in the forties—"
> "—taken that other job—"
> "—married him when I had the chance—"

The solution to ending your depression is a simple one; but it requires much effort on your part. And, of course, if you are depressed now, it is understandably difficult for you to try hard. But we challenge you to bring yourself out of depression by *Listening In, Stopping,* and *Switching.*

PETE'S DEPRESSION

Pete had lost the last job he held, and he felt it was because he had not done as well as he should have. He blamed himself for lack of a graduate degree, lack of drive, not being able to get along with his boss, not feeling comfortable with his fellow workers, and poor speaking and writing skills. The list was actually longer than that, as is typical of a seriously depressed person. He could list his shortcomings in excruciating and endless detail.

He had already been laid off before the stock market crash of 1987, so he had a very difficult time finding another job. The longer he was unemployed, the more depressed he became. It was hard for him to look through the papers to see what jobs were available. It seemed nearly impossible for him to send out his resume. He blocked when it came to phoning about a possible job interview.

After many months he started therapy. No one would deny that it is depressing to be unemployed. But as is the case with most depressives, he did not believe that he was causing his depression by what he was thinking. He thought he was being completely realistic in being depressed. Things were awful out in the real world. What did the therapist know about how depressing it was to be out of work? Wouldn't anyone be miserable if he had fouled up, the stock market crashed, and no one wanted to hire him?

Pete and his therapist worked on learning a new language, a language that did not produce nor reinforce depression. Pete had once studied French, and had spent a summer in France during his student days, so he could remember what it was like to speak a different language. It was this memory that helped him become an excellent student of Inner Speech Training. He used his previous language training to learn not to speak "Depression," and learned to speak what he simply chose to call, "Well-being."

This is the way Pete put it. "You have to think French words before you can speak French words. The English word occurs to you first, automatically. Then you stop that word, and switch to a French word. You have to go slowly at first because you can't come up with the French word that fast. The English word keeps going through your mind until you Switch it out. Then the French word finally comes through if you have studied the subject enough."

Pete continued, "When you are in the habit of speaking 'Depression,' that language will come up first in your mind. It takes practice; you know you don't want to speak 'Depression' anymore, so you switch it to 'Well-being' words."

Pete told this story about his experiences in searching for a new job. "I was sure I would foul up when I had a job interview. But I knew that sentence was spoken in 'Depression'—a language I didn't want to speak anymore. Those words would actually program me to do poorly. I had Listened In and heard the wrong language. I decided to speak the new language I was learning: I will prepare myself well. I will write out a few important things I want to say during the interview, and be able to say them confidently. That will help me to be more relaxed when I speak. I know that studies show that it takes about 20 interviews to get a job in my field at the salary I want."

His new language did help him to be far more self-assured. He thought something constructive, focused on what he could do, rather than what he couldn't do, and blocked out useless worry. He knew he would get a job after about 20 interviews, and he did.

As in learning to speak French, you can choose to say an English word or, with practice, you can eventually say a French word. That is a key concept in Inner Speech Training. Learning to speak any foreign language is basically the same as doing I.S.T. Most people will admit that they could take a course and eventually speak a foreign language fluently if they were exposed to it on a daily basis. But depressed people are very wary about believing that they could stop speaking "Depression," and learn to speak what Pete called "Well-being." Pete has now become something of a propagandist for I.S.T. His opening line to depressed people now is, "You always have the option of stopping the old words that have made you depressed. You can now choose to speak the words that make for well-being."

CHAPTER 16

THE DEFENSIVE–DETACHED THINKER
THE OFFENSIVE DEFENSE

In the classic story, a traveling salesman gets a flat tire on a dark, lonely road and then finds that he has no jack. He's delighted when he sees a light on in a farmhouse along the road, and he starts walking toward it. As he walks, his mind churns: "Suppose no one comes to the door." "Suppose they don't have a jack." "Suppose the guy is unfriendly and won't lend me his jack even if he has one." "I should have had my own jack." The harder his mind works, the more agitated he becomes, and when the door opens, he punches the farmer in the face, yelling, "You can keep your lousy jack!"

That story stays in people's minds because it represents a common type of thinking, something we all indulge in from time to time: defensiveness, and staying away (detached) from other people. This inner speech script is one in which we play two parts—our own and the other person's. Our Inner Voice plays a large part in the dialogue we invent. And so, in our script, the other guy is always unfriendly, angry, or accusing, and we're always justifying our behavior, defending ourselves, and thinking we should have stayed away from him in the first place.

We may not punch anyone, but we assault people verbally with a barrage of defenses. If you're a defensive thinker, you spend a lot of your time reacting to imaginary conversations. You think someone else's voice is always in your head, berating you. And you fill your mind answering the recriminations. "I couldn't help being late. There was an accident on the highway." "I didn't forget your birthday. The store was out of the right color in your size. They have to order it." Sometimes the excuses are in response to an actual complaint, sometimes merely to the voice in your head. Finally, you get exhausted and decide "People aren't worth it."

Defensive thinking is characterized by excessive explaining, in which your mind is forever justifying what you did or what you're about to do. It originates in defensive–detached persons because they think it is a hostile world out there, and they have to be ready at every moment to defend against the attack that is bound to come. Part of their defense is to be ready to justify everything they ever did. Part of the defense is to cover up and stay away from the supposed attackers. The effect of this defensive thinking is that the person refuses to be direct or to deal with the matter at hand. All this defending weakens a person rather than defends him. The very act of constructing excuses and explanations tires one out, and also makes one *look* weak. It's a case of "The lady doth protest too much."

The Offensive Defense of Rudolph

Rudolph was a brilliant scientist by the time he had graduated from college. His potential had been recognized when he was fourteen months old actually, when his parents discovered that he somehow could read the "Stop" and "Slow" signs in the street. He was placed in special schools for the gifted, and did brilliantly in every subject, but especially math and science.

He developed a personality that could readily be seen as defensive–detached. His relationships with his parents and also his siblings were distant and uninvolved. He developed a quiet aloofness, and seemed to others to have virtually no feelings about anything. He had an incredible command of the English language, and could fend everybody off with extremely logical arguments about why he was doing what he was doing, and why everyone else should leave him alone. In everything, he attempted to be entirely self-sufficient. He devised any number of schemes to insure his privacy. When he was urged to take up a sport, he studied all that were available, but was drawn only to individual rather than team sports. He settled on tennis. Then he decided to hit the ball against a blank wall rather than play with another person. With his mathematical mind, and his inner need to stay detached, he realized the ball would only go half as far if he hit it against the wall, and would come back to him in half the time, thereby allowing him to hit the ball twice as many times in a half-hour period. He could rationalize all this by saying that the purpose of exercise was to *exercise*, and he was only interested in doing it with optimum speed. Only much later was he able to see that his "efficiency" was essentially a defensive mechanism by which he avoided any involvement with another person.

Rudolph's personality had developed into a defensive–detached one very early. His parents often told the story that at the age of nine months he had thrown his bottle over the side of the crib in anger, and never sucked on a nipple again. He toiled-trained himself also at about nine months, and never wet a diaper or the bed again.

The origins of his patterns came about by an engulfing mother and father, probably from the time Rudolph was born. An older sibling had died in his crib before Rudolph was born, and the cause of death was never completely ascertained. When his precocious intelligence became known, he was hovered over even more, and he fought his parents off with an iron curtain of detachment and rapier-like responses. Generally, he tried to avoid verbal contact of a personal nature, because he felt he then stood less chance of getting pushed around, and he would suffer less.

After Rudolph finished graduate school, he started work in a research center. Even though his colleagues respected him, and recognized that he was a loner, certain demands were made on Rudolph to be a team player and communicate among peers during staff meetings. These were demands that he had largely been able to avoid throughout his life. As a result of his successes in navigating his way through life in a detached way, he had few social graces, and almost no ability to make small talk. He was inhibited, bumbling, often rude, and beneath it all, terribly fearful. As bright as he was, he knew that there was something seriously odd about him. He suffered less when he could make his detachment work for him, but he was extremely sensitive when he experienced how little basic self-esteem and self-confidence he had.

His inner turmoil and pain made him decide he had to do something about his condition. He wanted to do it all alone, as he had done most things in life. He read a number of books on neuroses, and diagnosed himself correctly. Next he wondered what kind of therapy would be best for him. He rejected anything that he considered "soft." He was a hard scientist himself and wanted a form of therapy that had been developed in the laboratory, or at least in universities and research centers. He decided cognitive restructuring fit his needs.

The basic thought in Rudolph's mind, the one that frightened him and produced the detached defensiveness, was the inner thought that contact with people would be destructive to him. Therefore, he had detached emotionally so he would feel less of the pain and danger connected with relating to people. The trauma of the original parent–child pattern was his expectation whenever he became involved with anyone, even another tennis player.

Listening In became a listening for the inner voice that said, "Don't tread on me." Any contact with another person, especially any advice, would cause him to become anxious. He did not know at first that there was a thought that preceded and caused the anxiety. When asked to find the thought that came first, he approached the task with the tools of a research scientist.

Soon he heard in his inner speech center, "Don't listen. They will take you over." He then learned to Underline "take you over." Then he Stopped that inner voice. He Switched to a phrase familiar to a scientist. He would think to himself, "Keep gathering data." That enabled him to keep his mind on what the other person was saying—the data—and he would remain objective long enough to withhold his anxiety. And then he would in time Reorient. He chose to Reorient by thinking that he was engaged in a 6-month research project to see if people were indeed as dangerous as he had felt them to be during his childhood. He had never really tested that hypothesis and decided that now was the time to do it.

He further Reoriented by deciding he would test his therapist, and his therapist's methods. He would put every Inner Speech Training Technique to a test. He was sure he could try each of the five I.S.T. techniques 20 times, and decide if they proved workable and useful. If he found that they worked more than half the time, then he would decide they were worth continuing. He held his therapist to very strict standards. The instructions he was to follow had to be specific and testable. Rudolph's I.Q. was probably about 30 points higher than his therapist's, but together they probably improved some of the methods that are now presented.

As Rudolph began to use I.S.T. successfully, he became more collegial and friendly. His detachment dropped away bit by bit with the therapist, and also with his colleagues, and eventually with the world at large. He met many turning points that helped him progress, but the basic leverage that he gained against his neurosis was when he realized that his anxiety and hypersensitivity were caused by an inner thought. This thought, he realized, continually worked to make him fearful of close encounters. When he discovered that he could challenge that thought, and that the thought was not necessarily accurate, he was on the road to changing his thought, then his feeling, and finally, his behavior.

CHAPTER 17

THE MEN'S PERSPECTIVE/
THE WOMEN'S PERSPECTIVE
OLD AND NEW THINKING FOR
MEN AND WOMEN

How do women and men think? And what do they think about that is important to their happiness?

Men and women have two major thinking preoccupations in common: Love and Work.

Women and men have two major emotional problems: depression and anxiety. Depression is a feeling of helplessness. ("Woe is me, all is lost.") Anxiety is a feeling that I am in danger of losing something I value as a human being. (Shakespeare wrote, "He who robs me of my good name—leaves me poor indeed.") In briefest summary, loss is at the heart of the feeling of depression, and danger is at the heart of the feeling of anxiety.

The origins of anxiety and depression are different for each person. However they may have been started, it is the thinking of the individual that now perpetuates those emotional problems. Men and women make the same type of thinking errors that can exaggerate and extend the depression and anxiety. Whether it is a man or woman, the anxious person is allowing thoughts of danger to fill the mind, and the depressed person is allowing thoughts of helplessness and hopelessness to fill the mind.

Many studies indicate that social factors—that is, receiving and giving *love*—are the major ingredients of happiness in both men and women. That means that two of the most damaging inner speeches one can have are, "I do not love" and "I am not loved." Those thoughts are danger signals.

An effective thinker will go to work with the intent to change and correct them. If you think that you are living a lonely life without love, it's time to Switch to different priorities: to learn to love, to find time to be with loving or potentially loving people, to enjoy sharing your inner speech. Loneliness has been described as the inability to share your deepest thoughts and feelings.

Working with this book you are becoming more aware of your deeper thoughts. Practice sharing them, and your intimacy with others will grow.

The second major thinking pattern that women and men share is *work*—or specifically, job satisfaction. It is a crucial component in the happiness of both men and women. Job satisfaction means primarily that a person values her/his work—whether it is inside or outside the home. Job satisfaction also includes freedom of work opportunity, a good income, growth potential, and vacations.

All this means that you will do well to Listen In to your Inner Speech and Underline when your job thoughts are a primary focus of grumbling and complaining. Monitor the job channel in your mind. If you hear words of misery, you are apt to be miserable. Given the importance of your work in your life, it is time to change—either your thinking or your job or, more probably, a combination of both.

So much for basic similarities in the thinking of men and women. What about the differences? While recent social developments have tended to lessen the role differences of the sexes, there remain both physiological and cultural differences between males and females that can lead to different styles of thinking. (Keep in mind though, that men and women use the same basic mechanisms. Therefore, the five basic I.S.T. methods work equally well for both women and men.)

For instance, research has demonstrated that females have more left-brain dominance. The left hemisphere is in charge of language, logic, and labels. Girls begin to think earlier and find certain school subjects like English and literature easier than boys do.

Further, the bundle of fibers that connects the two halves of the brain—the corpus callosum—is thicker in females than in males, suggesting that women may have a greater capacity to integrate the two hemispheres, combining right-brain visual and spatial abilities with left-brain verbal skills. Some people believe that this may form the basis for the greater intuitive skills in women.

Yet other research has shown a male–female difference in the control of aggression. After eighteen months of age, girls seem to gain better control over their tempers than boys. Of course, it can be argued that aggressiveness in a baby girl still shocks adults, whereas it may elicit approbative amusement in a boy— "What a little tough guy!—Hey, Slugger!" This may form the basis for the better verbal stress-coping strategies seen in women, as opposed to men, who are more likely to react to stress with physical aggression.

There still remain important differences in the social learning of girls and boys that lead to differing thinking patterns between females and males. No matter how much of a new woman, or a new man, you feel yourself to be, you will probably still see yourself in some of these familiar stereotypes.

Here are five popular stereotypes of what many men think about:

A man thinks—would *you* call it narcissistic thinking?

"To prove I am a *man*—I *must* be stronger, smarter, richer, and more sexually experienced than a woman."

What would *you* do if you were a man and you had a thought like that? You might begin by *Listening In* to what you are saying to yourself. An accurate appraisal of that sentence would surely cause you to Stop and Switch—to anything—anything to take some of that stress off yourself. *Reorienting* calls for you to picture yourself as a fuller person, dreaming other dreams, remembering pleasures in your life that didn't mean you had to outdo the woman in your life.

Don't be a victim of the male stereotype of the macho man.

A man might think—would *you* call this detached thinking?

"I *must not* depend on anyone for anything important to me—"

Underlining the *must not* will certainly point out that such thinking will ruin a relationship and make intimacy impossible. Such thinking could be subtitled "How to Grow an Ulcer."

Men do have many more ulcers than women. Since men think they should not depend on others, they go to a doctor less often than women, and when they finally do get to a doctor, their illnesses, on average, are more advanced than women's. As a result, a man's stay in a hospital averages 4 days longer than a woman's.

A man might think—would *you* call it obsessive thinking?

> "I must remain very rational. Stay cool, un-flappable, self-contained."

Wrong? Wrong! Get off it by *Switching*. Remember the joy of losing control in an orgasm—merging with your lover. That wasn't a "self-contained" moment.

New research is finding that men who are able and willing to share their feelings with others, and especially with women, have less heart disease and cancer. That "cool, self-contained" thinking style is costly when it comes to medical bills.

Some men think—would *you* call it defensive thinking?

> "I have to show them" ("them" meaning the *men* in the world out there).

So what really counts is getting your name in the paper? And what happens when your name isn't in the paper tomorrow or the day after? Who or what are you then? No one said it is easy to be a successful male or female these days—but look at the pressures you may be laying on yourself. Does your inner speech also go on to say something like, "It's the world out there that really counts. I am worth something when the world values me—with more acclaim, professional reputation, a larger income, more prizes. What I'm like inside the four walls of my home is pretty much hidden from the real world out there—so my private life doesn't count for as much."

Perhaps it is those thoughts about "I'll show them" that leads to the male style of aggressive driving on the highways. And what does it get men? Twice as many 20-year-old men are killed in auto accidents as 20-year-old women. And what about other forms of violence? Men are five times more likely to be murdered than women. And men, far more often than women, commit those murders.

Stop. What is there inside you that gives you pleasure? Try this exercise. Think for a few moments. Name the three most personally fulfilling experiences you have ever had. Not what *others* thought—but what *you* in your innermost self thought was truly fulfilling.

1._____ _____ _____
2._____
3._____

Think about those things.

Some men think—would *you* call this anxious thinking?

"I need to get ready for what's coming up."

Maybe you are one of the many males who is nearly always thinking, "I must prepare myself for what lies ahead. It doesn't matter how I feel right now.

It doesn't count whether or not I am enjoying myself now—it's piling up experiences for some future testing of me that really matters." Many men hardly live in the present at all—what really matters is how things are going to turn out, or so they think.

Men live 8 years less than women. There are many reasons for this. But certainly the man who thinks he must be tougher than others, not dependent on others, unfeeling, aggressive, is unwilling to live in the present and thinking primarily about the future—is setting himself up to die earlier than he would need to.

It's time to Reorient: Listen In to your best inner speech as you answer this simple question: "What do *I* really want?"

Now let us look at five of the old familiar thinking patterns among women.

Some women think—perhaps it is depressed thinking:

"What if I never meet anybody?"

Listen In to that one. It sounds like that woman (or is it a man?) is putting the source of her security outside herself, in someone else. What if? What if? That is risky, isn't it? Time to change, perhaps to something like, "I will become secure personally—inside myself. Then I will share that security with another person who is also secure."

Some women think—does it sound like masochistic thinking?

"I have to put him first."

Have to? His career, *his* well-being, *his* thin skin? Put them first?

Years ago little girls were raised to believe that they were to drop everything else when a man came along. It cost women the potential for their own strong identities. And it made men out to be the weaklings who couldn't survive without the "little woman" holding them together. How does this newer description sound to you? "We are equal and different." Have you Reoriented?

Some women think—might it be anxious thinking?

"I'm afraid I'll lose her as a friend."

That was said by a brilliant scientist, Wilma B., after she was offered a promotion. It meant leaving the lab where she and her colleague Ruth had worked side by side for three years.

Women have often felt that when they began to succeed in the marketplace they would become as competitive as men, and lose their valued relationships with their female friends. The old image of the "real" woman was that she was not to appear eager for success—it wasn't feminine. Underline your thought. Was it appropriate for, say, the Victorian era? Switch. It's a hundred years later. "I like using my brains, and it's great to be rewarded for how well I can do."

Some women think—does it sound like narcissistic thinking?

"I have the most beautiful body at this party.
But what will happen to me when I am older?"

This woman is thinking "a woman is her body." That is not unusual in our society. Never before has the exposed female body been so powerful. Glamor has become a woman's major asset. And many women have been taught to think that as their glamor fades, so does their identity. The culture of the time has dictated what kind of body has attractiveness and power: the fullness of the Renaissance, the hourglass shape of the Late Victorians, or the flatness of the current high-fashion magazines. In all of these, women were told how to shape themselves so they would have the "right" to think well of themselves.

It is time for this narcissistic woman to rethink her worth. Can she think she is more than the appearance of her body? Can she Switch to her inner self as a source of worth? The fashions will change. What catches a man's eye will change. The literature written now by thoughtful women provides valuable sources for a healthy sense of self based on talent, values, assertiveness, integrity, wisdom—all aspects of the self that grow with the passing years. They are assets worth thinking about when she prepares for the next party.

Some women think—does it sound like obsessive thinking?

"I'm not as good a wife and mother as my mother was."

Are you sure it is "not as good"? Could it be that more correctly you are a *different* wife and mother than your mother was?

More than 50 percent of wives are working outside the home today. Of course they will not do the same things their mothers did when they were full-time homemakers. Change your thinking to what you as a career woman can now offer your children, for example, in terms of a role model.

We could go on with these examples, and so can you. "I mustn't let anything compete with my loyalties at home. —I wish someone would take care of me. — How long can I go before I call him? —Do you think I said too much? —Was I too assertive? —Am I going to have to take care of myself all my life? —I never have enough time. —I wonder what others will think if I don't work outside my home." —Guilt. Guilt. Guilt.

Men's damaging inner speech most often occurs in relation to their position in the world, while women's inner speech most typically occurs in how they evaluate themselves in relation to their position with other people. (That is not the case for *all* men or *all* women.)

Listening In to women will help you underline how women often think about being a super-relater— succeeding in their relationships with both men and women (but especially with men) as a sign of self-worth. *Listening In* to men enables the listener to Underline the fact that men typically think of their self-worth in terms of how they succeed in the outside world. Witness the women's magazines: "Can This Marriage Be Saved?" And the men's magazines, "How I Shot the Big-Horned Elk."

What do these differences between men and women mean in relation to thinking?

The surprising answer is, not very much.

Thinking techniques work exactly the same for both sexes because both sexes think the same way. For women and for men, your awareness of your inner voice thoughts will help you effectively monitor your internal speech. You can Underline the weakening trends and Stop them. Thoughts and thinking are produced in both men and women in *the same way*—in words. You can hear the words. Decide if they are producing fear or depression. If they are, decide to change them to useful thinking. Change the words. Not falsely, but accurately in words that are helpful to you. Change your words and you change your feelings. Try it!

THE "HOW CAN I" TECHNIQUE FOR BOTH MEN AND WOMEN

Here is an effective technique that in a simple way will enable you to eliminate weakening thoughts.

Start by making a list of 10 of your most damaging thoughts. Some examples:

1. Things just don't go right for me.
2. How come I can't ever find the right job?
3. Nothing is ever enough.
4. I'm not relaxed with people.

Now you add some of your own special brand of damaging thinking.

Next, immediately switch these thoughts by adding just three words at the beginning of each sentence. The three words are "How can I."

"Things don't go right for me" becomes *"How can I make things go right for me?"*

"How come I can't find the right job" becomes *"How can I find the right job?"*

Do you see how you have Reoriented yourself from a helpless statement to a planning statement?

Finally, add two or three answers to each of your new "How can I?" questions. Don't stop with the questions. Add some answers that help you start doing something productive.

What are your answers to those four questions above?

    I can...

    I can...

    I can...

    I can...

CHAPTER 18

BETTER THINKING AND YOUR EVERYDAY PROBLEMS
STRESS, COPING, MIND-RACING, SEX, AND HEALTH

Whether you are a woman or a man, whatever type of basic personality you are, you face important everyday problems that require you to be at your best.

This chapter describes five important issues of daily living. To practice your thinking right now, try, as a case history is recounted, to devise your own solution before you reach the one suggested.

STRESS

The successful management of stress has become a major theme in our society. What you *think* can be either the greatest agent of stress or the greatest stress-reducer in your life.

Edgar's house burned down in the middle of the night. It was a frame house, and it burned to the ground except for the chimney. He and his family had been able to escape without injury, but the house burned so fast that they had been able to get nothing out of the house except four family photograph albums. It is difficult to imagine greater stress than to be awakened in the middle of the night by the sounds and heat and smoke of the house on fire, fearing for the lives of everyone in the family.

The next day Edgar was walking through the ruins of his house, suffered a heart attack, and died immediately.

The newspaper account said that he had spent the night at a neighbor's home and had left that house alone early the next morning to inspect his burned-out house. He was found dead a short time later. Police surmised that Edgar, a writer, had been surveying the charred remains of his books in what had been his study, where he usually wrote. It was there that he fell stricken, and his body was found.

We want to comment on this newspaper story (details have been changed) with caution. While we will never know what Edgar may have been thinking before he suffered a heart attack, we want to call attention to the fact that he survived the worst of the *physical* stress. That is, he escaped the fire of the night before. The next day, when he was inspecting his former home, it is likely he was thinking thoughts that caused him to experience enormous psychological stress. The heart attack came after the physical stress, but—again, this interpretation is just a possibility—perhaps during the worst of the mental stress.

A possible lesson to be learned is that in the midst of great external stress, such as the trauma of a fire, and following that stress, it is vital that one should Listen In to one's thoughts, so that those thoughts can be directed to center on comforting, quieting, and soothing measures, as far as that is possible to do. What you *think* is the *greatest stressor of all*; or, it can be a balm to you.

Students of I.S.T. have learned to think of themselves in a special way. They do not sneer at themselves. They do not stay mad at themselves. When they make an error, they encourage themselves. They remember that they did their best, given who they were at that moment. They weren't trying to make mistakes deliberately. Their thinking moves them ahead. They expect to build a more competent life.

How to Control Your Inner Dialogues to Reduce Stress

We live in a tense age. Stress permeates our lives in so many different ways that it is unusual when we aren't feeling some stress. Whether it is performing on the job, at a test, winning a game, or being in a relationship, we are surrounded by stress.

Where Do These Demands Come From?

The answer to that question should now come to your mind at once: from internal voices. These internal voices demand, demand, demand.

How Much Stress Are You Under?

Answer these 20 questions and you will get an effective measure of your reaction to the stress in your life.

Check the appropriate box:

       1=Hardly ever
       2=Occasionally
       3=Regularly
       4=Very often

Do you	Hardly ever	Occasionally	Regularly	Very often
1. Feel irritated or annoyed?	____	____	____	____
2. Get angry about little things?	____	____	____	____
3. Fly into a rage?	____	____	____	____
4. Forget things?	____	____	____	____
5. Have poor concentration?	____	____	____	____
6. Take too long to make a decision?	____	____	____	____
7. Perspire a lot?	____	____	____	____
8. Feel your heart pounding?	____	____	____	____

9. Experience that your muscles are stiff/tight? ___ ___ ___ ___
10. Feel faint? ___ ___ ___ ___
11. Find your hands trembling? ___ ___ ___ ___
12. Have an upset stomach? ___ ___ ___ ___
13. Feel nervous or tense inside? ___ ___ ___ ___
14. Avoid some things because of your fears? ___ ___ ___ ___
15. Feel you are losing interest in things? ___ ___ ___ ___
16. Have trouble sleeping and/or eating? ___ ___ ___ ___
17. Feel hopeless about the future? ___ ___ ___ ___
18. Feel lonely? ___ ___ ___ ___
19. Lack much sexual desire? ___ ___ ___ ___
20. Feel down? ___ ___ ___ ___

HOW TO SCORE YOUR ANSWERS

Now add your total score: If you had a "3" on the first question, and a "2" on the second question, your total score to that point would be 5. Continue until you have added the points for all 20 times.

If your total score was 20, you are kidding yourself.

If your total score was 80, we don't believe it. Someone with an 80 does not have the inner strength to be able to read this book and get to the end of a 20-item questionnaire.

But if you scored between 30 and 40, you are experiencing little stress in your life.

If you scored above 45, you need to think through what you are doing to yourself. Depending on how much above 45 your score went, you are in considerable distress, and even in danger of losing control of your mental health.

How you think about it determines the amount of stress that you experience.

Stress can be overwhelming at times, *but the essential and important difference is how you cope* with the stress. Stress does not necessarily lead to strain.

If you can control and handle your internal voices, you will be able to cope. It is very important to learn that halfway between the external stressor and your internal response, there is a *midway* point—a point where the stress can be handled, and where the real action is. The outcome of the midway battleground leads to productive living or it leads to anxiety and depression. Midway is where the voices are locked between the external stress—and what you think and do about it.

Outside stress eventually is changed into a *verbal*

thought in your mind. The stress comes to have a separate existence that you can perceive in your head.

But you can learn to *cope* with these verbal thoughts, these stressors, through improving your thinking techniques.

COPING

How often have you heard your own thoughts telling you unkind things?

"I don't think I want to try. I'll probably *fail*, then I'll just feel worse."

Like most skills, thinking takes practice. The skill that will help the thinker above is *Reorienting* to: "I will learn from the experience, even if I don't do it a hundred percent."
When your inner voice says

"Why go through with it? It won't make *any* difference..."

you are experiencing difficulties in your thinking.
Underline all the weakening words that are getting you into trouble. They are the words that rush to false conclusions. Your thoughts are actually *misrepresenting* your case—giving you *false information.*
It is time to Switch and think:

"Some things seem very difficult to me."

Now you have stopped thinking you are helpless. Now you can work out the several specific operations to be done to obtain a better rate of success.

Do you ever misinform yourself? Take Anita, a weekend tennis player who went out to hit the ball after looking at the professionals play at Wimbledon. An "easy" shot went out of bounds and Anita thought, "What's the use? I'll never be a tennis player!" Can you find the false information in her thought? Doesn't she really mean that she'll never control the ball like a champion? The pros practice three to five hours a day and have intensive coaching in each minute detail of the game.

Anita will feel better when she Switches to "I know I will play better if I take my racquet back sooner and have more time to stroke the ball."

Coping is defined as the way that you manage your problems. Your style of coping is the way that you deal with life—whether it is a flat tire, the death of a relative, or a rude waiter.

These styles of coping result from your mental patterning in the brain. They are developed originally early in your life to keep you feeling safe, secure, and comfortable. Your patterns of coping came primarily from how you learned to live with your parents and siblings. For the most part, you tend in adulthood to keep the same mental patterns and style that you used to get along in your childhood.

People cope in different ways and you can change your thinking to cope better.

If you want to see coping styles in action, watch a person with a flat tire during the rush hour on the San Diego Freeway (or the Northwest Tollway or the Long Island Expressway).

The Dependent Coper has his flat tire and sits in his car waiting for help to arrive.

The Submissive Coper waits, and when the police car arrives, he says to the officer, "Oh, officer, you police are the most wonderful people! Tell me what to do."

The Guilty Coper waits in his car for help to arrive. He then tells the arriving police officer, "Oh, officer, I have known this would happen. As you can see, one headlight is out, the brakes need relining, and I've only got one contact lens on. I mean, I'm a menace on the road."

The Dominating-Aggressive Coper strides to the nearest phone and calls the American Automobile Association, the highway patrol, and the state highway department. His shouted message to all three is, "You better get your trucks over here fast before I call the Governor. I pay my dues and taxes. These roads are a disgrace. Your service is outrageous, and your people are incompetent. I demand my rights."

The Withdrawal (Detached) Coper isolates himself. He abandons his car, climbs the fence to get out of the turnpike area, and walks home alone.

The Self-Image Expander announces to the policeman when he arrives, "My chauffeur was sick today so he couldn't drive me in my limo. My personal Mercedes is being delivered next week. So I borrowed this lemon from the dealer. And right away the tire blows on me. I've never been in a situation like this in my life."

The Healthy Character does whatever is appropriate safely to fix the tire and get himself on the way to his destination without undue delay or bother. He has a healthy self-regard which allows him to think that he can be interdependent with others and have the best of both worlds. Flat tires are a fact of life, and he knows he will manage.

Thinking underlies all these coping patterns. You gain power in your coping by *Listening In* and understanding which of these styles you typically follow.

You can gradually change your character pattern if you recognize it for what it is: a habitual mode of thinking that leads to habitual ways of acting.

You are about to have a job interview. Anxiety is normal at such a time. Here are ways to manage your thoughts:

Weak thinking	Inner Speech Training
"I *should have* dressed more conservatively. I *should have* looked up the history of this company."	"The job interview is today. I'll have an opportunity to discuss the situation and see if I want the job and if I'm suited to it."
Comment: Underline the weakening phrase, the critical voice.	*Comment:* This is a Switch to a productive thought.
"I'm *no good* at these job interviews. I *can't think* on my feet. I act like I'm *scared to death*."	"I learn something from every interview. By the time I've had 20 interviews, I will really know how to handle these situations."

Comment: Listen In. Is your inner voice critical or friendly? This voice is beating up on you.

"I wish I knew how to relax...."

Comment: Stop, Switch, Reorient. It's okay to admit you're still learning.

"Tensing up is a problem for me when I am interviewed. I know I will be anxious. I will just keep taking deep breaths, and think the word, 'relax.' To focus on the anxiety does not help me."

Comment: Listen In. Helpless thinking here. It provides no channels.

Comment: Nice Switch here. Start tackling the problems one at a time. If you know anxiety is the toughest one, concentrate on how you will handle the anxiety.

Many popular newspaper and magazine articles on stress write about *managing* stress. Rarely do they write about an in-depth understanding of the *causes* of stress. Economists are now recognizing that stress is a factor in many illnesses, in absenteeism, alcoholism, and drug abuse. It is estimated to cost our economy billions of dollars a year. Stress management programs in business and industry are increasingly popular, and millions of dollars are being budgeted to finance them.

Recently surveyed articles and programs on stress

management advocated throwing balloons around a room, attending lectures, telling jokes, eating a healthier diet, stopping smoking, doing aerobics, and walking away from the stressor. All of these suggestions are helpful in managing stress.

What all of these external activities miss is that stress is an internal condition which is primarily caused by the internal act of thinking. It is not the event, it is *what you think of the event* that causes, or does not cause you to experience stress in your body. Aerobics will get your mind off the stressors for a brief time, and that is important. Aerobics will also give you a physical feeling of well-being, and that is valuable. But no external activity will teach you how to Listen In to how you are converting an external stressor (e.g., the boss's angry memo) into an internal thought of helplessness or danger.

Reread the three dialogues above, which begin with weak thinking and then Switch into productive thinking. It may seem too simple; but it requires practice to make it effective. The point is not to deny that the boss wrote an angry memo. The next step is to take responsibility for your own thoughts in response to the boss's memo. You can think helplessly or constructively. You are then doing much more than "managing" stress, you are *reducing* it, and learning how to cure yourself of *allowing stressful thoughts* to run rampant in your mind.

The next time you read an article on stress, we suggest you add the techniques of Inner Speech Training. You will then work to eliminate the *cause* of stress in your inner speech, and develop those satisfying thoughts that help you gain control of your thoughts, your feelings, and your behavior.

MIND RACING

If you are going to cope better, one area to learn to manage is mind racing.

Everyone has experienced *mind racing* —when you can actually feel your thoughts speed up and pressure your mind. You can't prevent those thoughts entirely. They keep recurring. Mind racing can occur as your thoughts race backwards, trying to justify your actions of yesterday.

Things didn't go right yesterday. Your mind keeps trying to redo and undo the past. You keep hearing different alternatives.

"What if I hadn't?"

"What if I had just...?"

You can't let it go and you can't improve on it. Your racing mind is keeping you awake —painfully.

If you learn to control your thinking, you can fall asleep and not endlessly relive the pain.

Or even more exasperatingly, you have had a good day and have the prospect of an even greater day tomorrow —but you were so keyed up that your mind started racing, preparing for something that hasn't happened yet, until it was again the middle of the night and you couldn't fall asleep.

You have an important meeting tomorrow, but your mind keeps racing ahead, trying to anticipate how you will manage.

You think,

What will I do if...?

What will I do if...?

What will I do if...?

No matter what you do, you can't seem to shut down all the possibilities. Your mind keeps going, trying to solve a yet unborn world. And then, the next day you may be too tired to enjoy anything.

Of course, not all mind racing occurs at night. It's just that voice thoughts are more noticeable when your surroundings are relatively quiet.

All of us have shared the experience of accelerated thought processes, which occur in many ways under different circumstances. Occasionally they flood us with waves of creativity—too often escalating to the point where our thoughts become unmanageable.

Can you recall an instance when your mind racing prevented you from fully enjoying something?

Do you remember being like Althea D.? She was intellectually brilliant, but so busy worrying obsessively about the amount of work that she had to do for her examination that she kept on getting further and further behind. She thought about all the studying she had to do, rather than actually studying. Her mind kept going faster and faster until she was so out of control that she ran out of time to study for her examination.

Maybe you too can recall an instance when you had to juggle so many things in your mind that you ended up doing nothing right.

Whoever you are, whatever you do, you are probably victimized at some time by an inability to control the *speed* of your thoughts, to concentrate on any one task for an extended period of time.

Which of the following circumstances do you associate frequently with mind racing? We offer some examples. You may have some of your own.

	Never	Seldom	Fre-quently
1. Depression (I'm hopeless.)	____	____	____
2. Self-criticism (How stupid can I be?)	____	____	____
3. Anger (I hate, hate, hate.)	____	____	____
4. Sex (I can't get the memory of that time out of my head.)	____	____	____
5. Self-hurt and rejection (What's wrong with me? Men always leave me.)	____	____	____
6. Morbid pre-occupations (I'll probably die an early death.)	____	____	____
7. Free-floating anxiety (What if I can't breathe?)	____	____	____
8. Work situations (I'll never finish.)	____	____	____

9. Obsessions
   (Should I or
   shouldn't I
   call?)   _____   _____   _____

10. Performance
    anxiety
    (What if I
    don't pass?)   _____   _____   _____

11. Recurring
    fantasies (I'd
    like to tell him
    where to go.)   _____   _____   _____

12. Fear of failure
    (I won't be
    able to do it.) _____   _____   _____

13. Decision mak-
    ing (Should I
    change jobs
    now?)   _____   _____   _____

14. Premenstrual
    tension (I'm
    so sensitive to
    everything be-
    fore my
    period.)   _____   _____   _____

15. Excess stimu-
    lants (coffee,
    diet pills)
    (I have a buzz,
    or I can't stop
    my thoughts.)   _____   _____   _____

16. Sleep depriva-
    tion (insom-
    nia) (I'm
    exhausted. I
    can't control
    my mind.)   _____   _____   _____

THE PSYCHOLOGICAL CAUSES OF MIND RACING

Mind racing may be a manifestation of a particular style of personality. For example, an obsessive style is a type of thinking that won't let anything go.

When a particular drive or feeling isn't expressed adequately, a feeling of internal pressure develops. It is unfinished business that can cause the mind to race and obsessive persons often won't let anything get finished. What residues of frustrations continually plague you and weaken your power to think? Pinpoint those circumstances that are most chronically frustrating for you.

When a choice exists between two opposing forces, *conflict* develops. Certain situations can cause repeated conflict in the mind. A good example is family conflict. The person may be "caught" between the spouse and the parents. If this happens to you, you are the unwitting victim of two opposing forces that are using *you* as their battlefield. It is important to stop the battle.

Don't let yourself be a victim. Try to Brake and slow down the two or more different voices in your internal speech. After they are slowed down and more controllable, train yourself to stop them completely by substituting your *own* voice whenever possible.

Any mind may race when anxiety overflows—

either from an external crisis or an internal pressure. Anxiety registers in many different ways. Racing thoughts often lead to muscular tension. If you feel tension and stiffness in your muscles, alert your body's biofeedback mechanism. Use the *signal* of the muscular tension to alert yourself to slow your inner speech.

Visualizations (close cousins of *Reorienting*) are a useful technique to use with anxiety. Picture the anxiety-producing situation. See yourself in your mind as you handle it, coping with calm confidence.

A special type of mind racing occurs when your inner speech is in the form of a dialogue with *two or more voices* in your head fighting with each other. One frequently is the Superego—the attacking voice, full of self-put-downs. Another inner voice, we hope, is more reasonable. This raging between two parts of yourself can be controlled by changing your internal dialogues.

The young executive:

"I worry constantly if I should deduct more business expenses."

"Everybody does it."

HOW TO PREVENT MIND RACING

THE FIRST STEP

Identify the sources of your mind racing. Eliminate those precipitating ones that can be readily changed by physical means—like lowering coffee intake.

THE SECOND STEP

Be active. Challenge the problem. For example, if you find your mind racing chronically when you become angry due to repeated *frustrations*, try to work through the anger. Don't let it sit there. Be aware of it. Express it in a way that does not hurt others or you. If that is not possible, *displace* it onto something harmless—like ferocious exercise (an around-the-park run). It may then be easier to use I.S.T. You probably feel stronger after exercising. Then Underline and Switch the Weakening Words. Select more powerful words to control your emotions.

"He can't do that to me."

becomes

"How he treats people is *his* problem."

THE THIRD STEP

Decrease your muscular tension and you can relax and control your thinking.

The hidden principle is simple.

Tension (anxiety) is a state that is perceived and felt in the muscles of your body. If you can relax your muscles you can decrease the feedback from your body that fuels the pressure and the anxiety that you feel in your mind. People are frequently unaware that relaxation also travels *backwards* from your relaxed body back to your mind. Just as a relaxed mind helps to relax your body, so relaxed muscles will relax your mind.

SPECIALIZED WAYS OF REDUCING TENSION

1. CREATIVE EXERCISE

You've seen the joggers, the legions of runners. They know that proper exercise can be invaluable. It is one of the most important means of reducing tension, depression, and stopping your mind from racing. Today people are getting better faster by exercising properly. It doesn't have to be jogging, of course.

If you really have tension and want to get rid of it, you need to exercise—and exercise strenuously. No matter what else you do, you won't feel completely well until you exercise regularly.

The exercise needs to be strenuous enough to involve your cardiovascular system to the point that you increase your resting pulse rate. (The resting pulse is the pulse that is obtained 2 minutes *after* the exercise is completed.) The exercise should last 20 to 30 minutes, at least two to three times a week.

The remarkable, *paradoxical* fact is that the fatigue produced by exercise will make you feel less tired, rather than more tired. Finish your exercise with a few moments of I.S.T. Hear any weakening inner thoughts? Switch them. Exercise helps, but it will not keep you relaxed, unless you change your thoughts which produced the stress.

2. DRUGS

Drugs are only a *temporary* source of relief. They can help you bridge crises and stressful anxiety. They will not, however, make you think and feel better by themselves. (Note the sequence, thinking produces the feeling.) You need to work at it. This is especially true of tranquilizers that bring relaxation; after awhile they tend to lose their effectiveness. Used properly, they can be vitally important if you need a bridge—when you need to remember just how it feels to relax.

If you are using a tranquilizer, notice how you are able to get a little more "distance" on your problem thoughts with the help of the tranquilizer. You probably are still thinking the troublesome thought, but somehow it does not seem to be so terribly painful. If you can get some distance from your worries *with* a tranquilizer, you can learn to do it *without* a tranquilizer. Remember how you thought when you were on a tranquilizer? Then do the same thinking when you are not using the tranquilizer. It will give you a feeling of greater self-confidence when you can learn to quiet your thinking without resorting to any chemical help.

3. SPECIALIZED PSYCHOLOGICAL TRAINING

You can train your body to relax. Did you know that you can actually decrease the tension in your body?

Today, using advanced technical machines, you can feed back information from different parts of your body to your mind and train yourself to regulate those parts and functions of your body through the process called biofeedback.

Most of the work done today in biofeedback is in the area of muscular relaxation. This is the most important means of retraining your body to deal with a variety of dysfunctions like severe headaches, backaches, and colitis. It can be enormously effective if used properly. Biofeedback can help a wide range of disorders from your head (ache) to your toe (spasm). The biofeedback machine is signaling you when you are thinking the most useful thoughts to relax your body from head to toe.

The basic operation calls for a sophisticated machine to record and monitor the electrical activity of your muscles. You are given an electrical signal via feedback readings that tells you when your muscles are relaxed. Your mind then operates in a cycle with your muscles. As your muscles relax, your tension subsides. Your mind and body are being taught to work in a healing cycle.

Special training enables regulation of brain waves (alpha training), sweat glands, blood pressure, and heart beat.

4. SELF-TRAINING EXERCISES (SELF-RELAXATION EXERCISES)

Biofeedback is not the only way. Some of the same results can be produced with simple self-taught exercises. Nearly every self-help book includes them. Here is a basic example of an amazing 10-second exercise to relax and feel better.

> Ready...Flex your arms and your legs. Tighten *all* the muscles in your body and hold them for a count of 10. Then count backwards from 10 as *slowly* as possible, gently releasing your muscles. You will immediately sense a

wave of relaxation spreading over the muscles
of your body.

Repeat this exercise several times. Each time, you will
feel more relaxed. The incorporation of such a simple
exercise into your daily routine will decrease the tension you feel. Do it several times every day! Couple the
exercise with Inner Speech exercises. Learn to Switch
to those relaxing thoughts.

Everyone has been told countless times "just relax," in the dentist's chair, when starting a new job,
when walking down the aisle to be married. But like
the weather, no one has *done* much about relaxation. It
has not been scientifically possible to teach people how
to relax so that it became a lasting response. Saints and
geniuses throughout history have mastered the techniques themselves, but their success may have been
due to their special gifts.

Now relaxation is getting a lot of much-needed research, and for good reasons. Relaxation improves the
body's immune system, lowers the heart rate and blood
pressure, slows the brain waves, reduces pain in most
instances, and often relieves gastrointestinal discomfort.

In keeping with the focus of the present volume,
we want to alert you to the importance of your thinking
in promoting your own relaxation. It is what you think
about that relaxes you, or prevents you from relaxing.
The thoughts in your mind make it happen. It is crucial
for you to Stop and Switch from your everyday worries,
concerns, and preoccupations if you want to learn to
relax. Then you can allow space in your mind for those
quieting, calming, tranquilizing thoughts that block
the chemicals in your brain that pump up your stress
level.

Choose right now, as you think about learning how
to relax, a short phrase or word that is very calming to
you. Say or think the phrase to yourself several times.
Now exhale rather slowly, and repeat those calming
words as you exhale. A helpful phrase will be one that
reminds you that you are safe, secure, and stable. Pick
a phrase that confirms that you are all right, that your
future is going to be all right. Many people choose a
meaningful phrase from their religious tradition. Be
sure that for you they are words that connect and reso-
nate deeply within you. Combine those words with a
quiet breathing out. It is breathing out that relaxes you,
far more than breathing in. Slowly, easily, think and
breathe. Think and breathe.

An effective way to Stop and Switch from your
tensions is to picture your muscles systematically relaxing. Start at either end of your body and think your way
to the other end, naming the sections of your body and
thinking about them relaxing. Thinking about your
muscles relaxing will silence the static in your mind,
and enable you to Switch to your thoughts and your
body working in concert to bring on the feeling of well-
being.

Keep out the bothersome thoughts by concentrat-
ing on affirming thoughts. Breathing has an automatically calming effect, but much more so if you combine
it with a quiet thought reflecting a solid, strong integra-
tion of your best self.

This form of systematic relaxation will be more effective as you practice it. Intruding thoughts will occur,
and you will discover how you can let those interrup-
tions pass right on out of your mind without becoming
upset about them. As you enjoy the calming effects of
your systematic relaxation exercise, you will find that

relaxation can be even more calming than sleep sometimes is. Sleep can, at times, even interfere with relaxation when it is a sleep troubled by unpleasant dreams.
You probably have had occasions when you awoke and
felt you had been working hard most of the night as
you slept. Relaxation can be under your own control,
whereas some sleep is not under your control. That is
why we know that relaxation exercises can contribute a
special benefit to you. Try it, 10 minutes a day and find
out for yourself.

SEX

You are only as sexy as you think. As unlikely as it
seems, your mind is the main sexual organ of your
body. Thinking is what produces sexual arousal. Or-
gasms are not caused by the genitals, but by the cere-
bral cortex.

Your sex life is that part of your life that is probably
the most convincing proof that what you think causes
what you feel. You know what it is like to feel sexy. Try
this exercise: try to feel sexy as you reread the previous
paragraph. Just keep reading. You are reading a section
of this chapter that is about sex. Now stop the exercise.
Did you start feeling sexy? Probably not. You were
reading sentences about sex, but these sentences were
not sexy. Feeling sexy is a by-product of thinking sexy
thoughts. Now think some sexy thoughts. Take a few
moments and think of one of your favorite sexual fantasies. Let your fantasy go on for a few minutes. Now
stop the exercise. If you were able to get into your daydream, you probably began to feel sexy.

You have just read the key to a better sex life: think sexier thoughts.

You can have intense sexual experiences from reading erotic literature through thought. Visual stimulation can lead you to feel sexual pleasure. Strong fantasies and daydreams can induce an intense state of sexual arousal even without physical stimulation.

On the other hand, thoughts can stifle sexual arousal.

> "I'm so afraid that I won't come that I don't even want to have sex."
> "He (She) turns me off."

STOP!

Only you can turn yourself off...Here is one way to fail:

> "*Nothing* makes me feel good sexually."

Your body has sensitive nerve endings which are concentrated in the sexual erotic areas.

You *can* feel, but your thinking may Switch to produce anxiety, rather than sexual pleasure.

If during lovemaking you keep thinking about how you are "performing," your thinking will almost certainly cause sexual problems. Thoughts like, "Does he like what I am doing?" or "Can I hold out long enough?" will cause you (and maybe your partner) to "turn off." If you think: "Does he (she) like me? or "My penis (breasts) are too small," your anxiety level will skyrocket and sex will be no fun. While you need stimulation of your sexual organs and other erogenous zones to achieve orgasm, you also need to have pleasurable, exciting thoughts during sex and to eliminate weakening thoughts.

Switching from your present sexual distracting thoughts can produce a wider and more intense sexual world for you that may have eluded you previously.

Listen In to the natural flow of the body. Concentrate by *Reorienting* the focus onto the sexual language of the body and mind. The capacity to be aroused fully is in you. Let your mind just listen to your body. Think about what your body is saying.

An important question you can ask while making love is, "What feels better...?" Keep asking yourself if there is a way that your lover can interact with you to make you both feel *even* sexier. Then do it.

Reorienting is a natural, and loving, lovely way to enjoy sex—if you leave yourself free to concentrate to do it. Use a number of reorienting questions to help you.

For example, ask yourself, "What thoughts are sexy?" Ask yourself, "What feels good?"

Hear the answers from your own mind and body. A mutual exploration will then lead you to develop a *style of lovemaking* that will enable you to reach greater sexual arousal and fulfillment. By "mutual exploration" we mean *talking* out your sexual preferences as well as acting them out together. With all the courage you can muster, tell your partner what you like best about being together with him/her sexually. Be tactful. Don't criticize; say, "I really like doing this, let's do it longer. And let's add some more of that." Express your appreciation of your partner's sexiest efforts. Compliments are always a stimulant. The greatest aphrodisiac is the warmth of a lover's responses. Human love can speak as well as show itself.

Your specific sexual interests are as unique as your thumbprint. No one else in the world has exactly your version of your sexiest daydream. There is no way that your partner is going to be able to guess what is the best way to turn you on—unless you have the openness to tell him/her.

Susan discovered that when she was getting very close to a climax, she wanted her husband to be completely motionless, and just hold her. When he did that, she almost always let go and had an orgasm. The point of this particular case illustration is that her husband would never have known exactly what she needed for sexual fulfillment unless she had told him. If she had not asked for what she wanted, she would probably have continued to feel frustrated and perhaps angry at her husband, and he would have felt that she was an unresponsive lover. Gently, lovingly, tell your partner about what is sexy for you in your thoughts.

A technique that will help you Reorient your sexuality is the *visual walk-through*.

Here is the way you do a sexual walk-through: You are now going to be the producer, director, author, and actor (and the entire audience) in the most erotic sexual encounter that you can imagine.

Start out by seeing a picture of the beginning of an ideal sexual encounter—anything you want. You have complete control. You are going to be able to do everything you have ever wanted to do. Now let the cameras roll. Add the details that excite you. Redo the scene if you would like to intensify a part of it. Keep going. You are being told how marvelous and exciting you are, that your lover has dreamed of this. As you continue with this fantasy of yourself making love, you are developing new thoughts that free you sexually.

Keep at these sexual walk-throughs. Add to your script. Make it more loving, more exciting, more fun. You will enjoy *being* a better lover as you mentally rehearse how to go about being a satisfying and satisfied lover. By doing these sexual walk-throughs you are grooving your mental pathways, so they will roll that much smoother the next time you make love.

Remember to Switch.

If you keep yourself aware of your internal speech and listen carefully to your thoughts, you can Underline the negative, critical, and irrelevant thoughts. If you keep hearing an obstructing voice cutting into your pleasant thoughts—get rid of the takeovers. Switch back to your most erotic thought-stream.

BARBARA, GENE, AND SEX

Barbara R. was 28 years old, had been married for 5 years, and was dissatisfied with her lovemaking. She was not only very tense and anxious while making love, but very angry at her husband, Gene, about her lack of sexual fulfillment. She felt that he had failed her, and that she had failed herself.

Her lovemaking did get worse as her thinking worsened. She grew angrier and more upset. When she had a sexual feeling, almost immediately she would think *negative thoughts* about Gene and their attempts to make love. Angry thoughts about past wrongs automatically intruded on her.

She knew that her angry thoughts were interfering with her sexual pleasure, but she felt that her thoughts got control of her and there was nothing she could do about it. She became very self-conscious when she tried

to make love. She tried as hard as she could to do everything right. Books on sexual technique helped her
some. But the harder she tried, the more she kept
thinking about how she was doing. She developed performance anxiety. She had read a lot about performance
anxiety, but she did not seem able to stop thinking
about how she was performing in bed. She felt trapped.
The more she thought about sex, and studied sex, the
less sexy she felt when she got into bed.

She wanted to change. She was sophisticated
enough to know that it wasn't all her husband's fault.
"It takes two." She had read that often enough to know
that it had to be true.

In time, she learned to Switch the voices in her
head. She Stopped thinking about sex, and began to
think sexy scenarios. She practiced and eventually succeeded at *Stopping* and *Switching* out the angry
thoughts about her past sex life. She decided it was of
no use to remember angry memories about Gene when
what she really wanted to do was to make exciting love
with him. He wanted the same. They both knew their
marriage was not perfect, but they loved each other underneath the accumulated anger of their years together.
And so they realized they were seriously shortchanging
each other by bringing their anger into the bed.

Two changes in her thinking were the keys to Barbara's increased sexual enjoyment. She listened to her
body, and this helped her Switch to sexier thoughts.
And she developed new thoughts. Anger at Gene during sex had become a habitual, automatic thought.
While her anger did not immediately subside, she realized she could stop the angry thought when it rose to
her mind. She learned to Switch to some things about
her husband that she *liked* when making love: Gene had

an anxious, hopeful way of looking at her that was sweet, he had wide shoulders and a good tight midsection. When she did that, she learned to think about more sexy thoughts, and then grow progressively less angry at Gene, because she was enjoying more sexual pleasure. As their sexual life improved, they found it was worth the effort to try to develop improvement in other areas of their relationship as well.

You can rewrite the script of your sex life. Just work with your most important sexual organ—your own mind.

PHYSICAL HEALTH

Can happy thoughts make you physically healthier? The mind affects the body, but does the mind control the body? The answer is growing more affirmative, as science discovers how the mind, and especially thinking, exerts its influences on disease and health.

The relation of stress to illness has been widely known since the discovery that the blood cells that counteract disease cells are less active in the bodies of persons who have recently lost a spouse. The body is physically less resistant to illness (in a biochemically measurable way) following a stress that involves an important loss (a loved one) and puts new pressures (the prospect of living alone) on the survivor. Since the original research on widows and widowers, other studies have added information that many of the traumatic events in life (loss of a job, failure in school, loneliness) decrease the activity of the immune system, and lead to more illness.

Stress, of course, is in the mind of the beholder. What may be stressful for one person is fulfillment for someone else. A politician may be distressed when he has no opportunity to speak in public. The new president of the P.T.A. may be panicked when he or she must give a speech at the first public meeting. Again, it is not the event, but what one thinks of oneself in the face of the event that determines the degree of stress. If one thinks of oneself as capable and competent, the stress response is minimal, and the immune system is little affected.

So stress, like relaxation, is a response produced in large measure by what one thinks about. A generally stressful event, when it leads to panicky thinking like "How am I ever going to manage now?" will make one prone to illness.

What about the reverse? Will thinking cure an illness already in progress? The evidence now is strong that one's thoughts and attitudes can affect illness, and increase the effective activity of the immune system. However, only a few scientists who have studied statistical data carefully are fully convinced that thoughts and attitudes will cure a serious illness already under way. Nonetheless, nearly everyone has heard stories of recovered patients who attribute their health to their own resolve to fight their disease with a combination of psychological measures in cooperation with their doctors.

There is some research that has indicated that people can strengthen their immune systems by visualizing the white blood cells engulfing the germs in the body. People who have been taught systematic relaxation, followed by imaging themselves more strong and fit were able to increase the effectiveness of the immune system. Women who are angry about their breast cancer, for example, and fight it, also increase their chances of survival because their attitudes seem to mobilize their immune functions. More research is under way, and the results are promising.

There are many ways to treat an illness, and years ago they would not have been considered part of the medical treatment. These extra treatment methods go by the name of complementary medical care. Under medical supervision, these methods may include some or all of the following: a healthy diet, appropriate exercise, nutritional supplements, the use of humor, psychological counseling, relaxation training and possibly biofeedback as well, meditation, medical and spiritual support groups, and imaging.

The thought that one has some control over one's life circumstances gives hope, and hope leads to motivation. The expectation of success increases the chances of success. A study of the elderly in a nursing home found that those persons who had a hand in choosing their menu, their clothing, even the color of their rooms, would live longer than those who had no such control of their daily lives.

It's not all in the mind, of course; but the active participation of the patient in the healing process will probably influence the quantity of the patient's life — and it undoubtedly will help improve the quality of that life.

Perhaps you cannot think yourself completely well, but you can think yourself better.

CHAPTER 19

THE ACCOMPLISHED THINKER — YOU
PRODUCTIVITY AND CREATIVITY THROUGH YOUR OWN THINKING

You have discovered that it is possible to change your life by changing your thoughts. How you *think* about your life determines how you *feel* about your life.

You have an internal dialogue that is alive and active every day. This dialogue is composed of your thoughts. Your thoughts judge your thoughts, they judge you.

Although it is outside the scope of this book to describe where and how in early childhood you developed your own unique internal dialogue, you as an adult can take charge of that dialogue.

Near the end of his life, Winston Churchill said, "All the dreams of my youth have been realized." Even Churchill could have chosen to think, "I am no longer virile and strong, I am about to die. It is the end for me." Both statements would have been true. Which thought he chose to think made the difference in what he felt.

You can be conscious of what you think.

When you learned to drive an automobile, you thought of every move you made. Now you rarely think consciously when you drive, because it is so easy for you.

But if you went to England, and drove a car with the steering wheel on the right side, and drove on the left side of the road, you would be very conscious of your thinking again.

You can become conscious of your thoughts. If there is some part of your life that you want to change, change your thoughts, just as you would change your thoughts to drive a car in England.

If anxiety or depression are what you want to change, concentrate on hearing internal thoughts of danger or significant loss that lead you to be anxious or depressed. It's Technique #1: *Listening In.*

PRACTICE THINKING IN SLOW MOTION

You will then hear your voice thoughts more clearly, become more aware, and change your thoughts when you want to. If you practice thinking more slowly, you'll be able to separate each word as it goes into forming your thought. This ability to separate the components will give you more powerful thinking. It's Technique #2: *Underlining. While many thoughts are true, only some are helpful.*

You have the choice of avoiding many truthful thoughts that are of no present value to you. It's Technique #3: *Stopping.*

WHAT IS USEFUL TO THINK ABOUT?

As you think about the words on this page, it is not useful to dwell on every conceivable danger that could possibly befall you: cancer, nuclear fallout, a stock market crash.

If you are actively working on those problems at the moment, of course it is helpful to think about them. But if your present task is to tuck your two children into bed, then choose the best framework of useful thoughts of wanting the best for those children, and helping them to attain it.

It is not useful to regret the past, if you dwell only on the regret.

It can be useful to think of your errors if you focus now on what you can do and will improve next time.

Habitual self-critical thinking becomes a self-fulfilling prophecy. A person will develop a sequence of self-attacks that are almost as familiar as the sequence in brushing one's teeth. "I have trouble with math," is probably paired with thinking, "I have the worst time balancing my checkbook; I'm no good with money when it comes to figures; I'll never be able to understand the stock market; I'll never be rich." You can see how one thought leads to another in this chain of put-downs centered on numbers. Self-critical thinking can be an expensive habit!

Whether your boss bawls you out, or your inner speech bawls you out, the inner response is much the same: blood pressure rises, acid in the stomach flows faster, arteries tighten. This is the body's normal reaction to stress. If the stress lasts long enough, or switches on and off enough times, exhaustion occurs.

It may save your life to stop the self-critical thinking that produces your stress reaction. That takes some changes in your thinking, but the stress and exhaustion caused by your internal attacks on yourself are worth learning to avoid.

In general, it is *not useful to worry*. Worry has a future orientation and you are living in the here and now.

Albert Einstein said he had his most creative thoughts while shaving in the morning. How do you do your creative thinking? Each of us thinks creatively in some particular way every day—probably not the same way Einstein did.

Too often we are put off by the seemingly facile way in which outstanding creative people seem to operate. They make it seem too easy.

"Just as I was boarding the morning bus, the theory explaining the ultimate quantification of the universe based on a twelve tonal note system came fully into my mind—I stopped to jot it down on my bus ticket."

This fools us by somehow hiding all the months of hard work that preceded the breakthrough.

But even though you may not make an important discovery of public importance, you can create the shape of your own life—and that is no mean feat.

Stretch your imagination and develop your capacity to be creative in numerous small ways—a better route home, a new diet, changing a color scheme, terrific lovemaking. This is Technique #5: *Reorienting*.

How can you help yourself creatively in terms of your daily life? Here's an example: Instead of being trapped by the same boring routine everyday traveling to work, your imagination can create rich, vivid stories about the people and places you pass.

Train yourself to practice by making up the wildest imaginable story about the most colorless person in your day.

Try it several times a day. Has your day suddenly become more interesting? Go a little further. Imagine more interesting people. Let yourself have imaginary conversations with them.

WHAT IS CREATIVE THINKING?

Creative thinking is thinking that goes beyond established order and views the universe, or some part of it, in a new and different way.

Think thoughts that get behind the surface appearance of things. Some people think, "I hate the city." Someone else thinks on a more creative level like this: "I dislike the city because it limits my chances for outdoor exercise." This thought is specific, it indicates what the problem is, and points to a possible solution. The next thought might be, "I will investigate one different city park a month for the next year, and see what I could do that would be fun in those parks."

Leave your options open as you think. "I don't think I will ever be able to afford a trip around the world." That certainly is not a useful thought and, besides, it probably isn't even true. Try this more creative thought: "With air fares coming down, with more charter flights and vacation club plans, some day I might be able to make a round-the-world trip."

Too many people choose thoughts that eliminate even the possibility of creating a creative thought.

Thinking creatively is the ability to express yourself freely to a fuller potential, both internally and externally. It begins with your thoughts.

WHY SHOULD YOU BOTHER TO LEARN HOW TO THINK MORE CREATIVELY?

The process of thinking creatively leads to a deeper feeling of living a fuller and more satisfying life. Or being totally absorbed, losing a sense of time, having the freedom and capacity to see a different world and to be different.

Take every opportunity to be creative even when it is only in the most minor way in your everyday life. Seeing something familiar differently—a flower, a tree, a building, and reorganizing your everyday associations.

The important news is that thinking can be designed to allow more creativity. Thinking creatively involves far more manageable processes than waiting for that bolt of lightning. Creativity can be improved with practice and awareness in stages.

THERE ARE SEVERAL STAGES

1. *Observations* of the *need* for something new and different—"I read that the world may run out of oil in the future."
2. Now the *need* has to be *analyzed* and different patterns observed—"Can our present supply be used more effectively or do we need new types of fuel?" Then the person needs *to find the clue* that suggests where the answer can be sought. This step works best when the seeker actively *challenges* the existing material.

    "Engines are grossly inefficient. Is there a *new* way to build a more efficient engine with less heat loss?"

3. Finally, when the imagination begins to flow, the thinker comes up with what is termed lateral thinking—thinking that doesn't close down any associational possibilities. It's Technique #5: *Reorienting*.

At first, "brainstorm"—considering, perhaps even writing down, any solution that comes to mind, no matter how zany or farfetched. Then eliminate what is impossible. What you have left is the "possible." Choose the best and try it out. Disconnect old habitual thoughts and feelings so that new associations can form more freely, and try to see all the new connections (although some of the process seems to be below the level of conscious inner speech). Mixing hard-nosed research with free-floating divergent thinking is the best use of creative time.

Don't Select the Same Thoughts Over and Over Again

If you are thinking about a problem and find yourself coming back over the same thoughts, *reroute your thinking*. When you Listen In and hear repetitions, it's a sign that you are not advancing; *your choice of words has trapped you* in the same spot.

Train your inner speech not to use clichés, because they indicate that you are not thinking *actively*. As soon as you discover that you are covering the same ground again by using the same words, let it be a signal to you to *select* a different set of thoughts. This will ensure that you have new ideas. Obsessive, ruminating, circular thoughts are a diagnostic sign of rigid thinking.

Rigid thinking ultimately becomes self-defeating thinking.

Inner Speech Training emphasizes this principle: As soon as you realize you are having weak thoughts that you had before, accept the fact that (for the present moment) you are not making progress. Select new words and thereby change the subject in your mind, or take a break and come back to the problem later when you have a new mindset. You may think it is avoiding the issue. This is not so. Repetitious thinking means that you are not getting anywhere. It is more efficient to Reorient yourself and come back to it later. In the meantime, your unconscious will be working for you. Your unconscious is incubating new thoughts.

HOW CAN WE WORK WITH OUR INNER SPEECH TO ENHANCE OUR CREATIVE ABILITIES?

1. *Change your voice thoughts to decrease your inhibitions and take a new look at things.*

Stop those Weakening Words that lead to negative self-criticism. "Oh, I'm no good at that." What possible value does that negative commercial have? None. It is both boring and useless.

You don't need all those voice thoughts that tell you you can't do something.

If you think, "I *won't* take a vacation this year," you change your whole viewpoint from what it would be if you thought, "I *can't* take a vacation this year." You will feel more powerful if you *create a choice.* Use words that indicate *you are never finished* — that *your possibilities have not come to an end.*

A powerful technique that is frequently used in

groups is to change "I will try" to "I will." This is a basic change in cognitive style that keeps the potential alive.

Practice thinking

"What can I do?"

Practice Switching when you hear...

"I don't know if I can do that..."

What would you Switch to?

"I can..."   "I will..."

It is important to realize that what you do is a choice, not a "have to."

As soon as you train yourself to select a thought that indicates to yourself that *nearly everything you do in life is a choice*, you will experience new creativity in your life and not be imprisoned by weakening thoughts, words, and actions.

2. *Build up your creative courage.*

There is a newness and challenge to every creative encounter. Erich Fromm speaks of "creative courage" as that quality that allows one to reach out and encounter change. Remember that freedom is victory over fear.

To be creative in your thinking, reach out *actively* and focus on what you want to encounter.

3. *Take a creative break.*

Devote a part of your day to creative thinking. Call it daydreaming if you prefer. Think out loud if that helps you.

If you want to be an astronomer, practice thinking about the skies and the galaxies—not the rent.

Internal stimulation is the knack of *using your own thinking* to think about the things you want to do. A potential scientist can't linger all day thinking about where she parked her car. A new office manager can't be creative if he worries all day long about whether that day-old cough is the first sign of a fatal disease.

List the *potentially* creative people you know. Can you spot their creative blocks? How do they frustrate themselves? What are the weaknesses in their thinking? Any similarity with your own procrastinating? Learn from watching.

> ...Creative job shapers
> ...Creative planners
> ...Artists, sculptors, fledgling novelists
> ...The plain person with the good mind who seems to find a way to solve problems at work. How does she/he think?

4. *Remember that the imagination is the outreaching of the mind.*

Don't be threatened by strange voices or new directions in your thoughts. Practice visualizations to expand your imagination. Try to put together visually the wildest, most discordant elements—grass in the middle of skyscrapers, a television set placed in the middle of the ocean. And then practice uniting these thoughts with a discovery—a particular pattern. Your imagination can be expanded with practice.

5. *The too-bad-we-were-overtrained theory.*

Too much of our adult world is overcontrolled and overmanaged. Too much fun has disappeared—a victim of "overtraining." Frequently, the most creative periods of our lives are during adolescence, when our thinking was flowing and we were less inhibited by a sense of the way things ought to be. We hadn't yet learned all the "musts" or "buts." Our thinking hadn't become: "We never did that before, so let's not do it now."

"It's no use—nothing creative happens."

STOP!! SWITCH!

"I'm learning to become more creative."

Fear forces your thoughts to march in the same old ruts. Go beyond your old self.

"It's never worth the time."

STOP!!
SWITCH!

"I'm going to invest some time in this. It may prove worthwhile."

6. *Don't use the thoughts "all," "nothing," "every," "none," "never," "always."* The rule is to avoid *universalizers* and *generalizers* in your vocabulary.

"I lead such a boring life, I *never* do anything creative." Do you *really* mean that you don't do *anything* creative?

7. *Don't use tyrannical imperatives.*

Simply eliminate from your vocabulary *"should/ must/have to."* Those words tyrannize you, and tyranny doesn't work. It breeds resentment, rebellion, and obstinacy. That may stop you from having the fun of being creative.

Negative internal voices erode the power in your

mental processes and prevent you from realizing the unique, exquisite pleasures of being creative. Negative voices limit freedom by condemning the proposed goal before it is even born.

Don't subtract from a positive statement ("butting in").

Therefore, rarely use the words, "but/however/except/on the other hand."

Don't "butt in" and interrupt a positive statement by compulsively linking a negative statement.

"I got good grades—*but* I was really lucky."

"I enjoy getting out into the country; *however*, I don't do it often enough."

"I love good music; *however*, I should really have learned more about it."

"In one way, I'd love to do it; *on the other hand*, it could present problems."

People with weakening ambivalence in their inner speech won't say something positive about themselves *without* following it with a subtraction. Some people can't hear a compliment without changing it: "Your hair looks great today." Their inner speech follows with, "It looked stringy yesterday."

If you will carefully avoid certain roadblock words like "but/except/however," your inner dialogues will lead to less self-defeat and to more creative options. Don't "undo" the first half of a creative sentence in your mind. You can keep your creativity flowing like a river, if you do not dam it up with a "but."

Thinking is a thrilling and exciting endeavor in and of itself, when you don't cut it off with some sabotaging thought. Your thinking is the royal road to creativity: let it *flow*.

CONCLUSION

INNER SPEECH TRAINING REVIEWED
FIVE STEPS TO HEALTHY INNER SPEECH

By now, you have started to notice how people around you handle their thinking. Ask yourself which ones make repeated errors—think thoughts that weaken their lives. Even more importantly, try to notice the positive people in your life. How do they think? Just what is it that makes them so chipper, so stimulating to be around? Try to figure out exactly what great thoughts are in their inner speech. *Ask* them.

Ask some friends if they notice what causes their feelings to *change*. Do people around you know that they begin to feel morose because they just had a thought that they lost or are missing something in their lives? Do they know that a sudden panicky feeling was brought on by their thought of some danger they thought they couldn't handle? Comparing notes can be a great mind expander.

Right now is a crucial time for you. For this system to be of maximum value in your life, you need to keep thinking about it. Keep LISTENING IN, UNDERLINING, STOPPING, SWITCHING, REORIENTING.

Remember that how you think can weaken or strengthen your whole life. So keep referring to these ideas. They can come to have more and more meaning for you. Select and underline passages most helpful for your thinking. Check the ways you have already improved. Make a note to yourself about the problem areas that remain.

And this is only the start of your new thinking. As H.G. Wells reminded us, "The past is but the beginning of a beginning."

INDEX